WISE DON'T ADVISE

NOT ANOTHER SHELF-HELP BOOK

HARSHA VARDHAN JANGAM

Dedicated

To my father,

who gave me life, love and letters

Contents

Contents

Foreword

Before you begin…

This is not the book of answers to your questions, nor the clarifications for your confusions, nor it gives ready-made solutions for your problems because solutions are not like COVID-19 vaccines, not the same for everyone.

The book just enables you to question the answers, doubt your conclusions and thereby clarify your confusions. It's all about evoking the right thought process.

Through real-life experiences, examples and experiments, the write-ups in the book take you through different points of view and stands.

The best way of getting clarity on any matter or opinion is to get more confused, just like running in a maze, seeming to reach the exit but going inside. We eventually come out at the end, but the beauty lies in the confusion midway.

The book talks about many challenges we face – jealousy, pain, possessiveness, rejections, revenge – and the root of all these: ego.

Happy reading!

CHAPTER ONE

POSITIVE JEALOUSY

He is taller than me. She has got golden brown eyes. He's well-built. What an amazing smile she has got! He is so handsome. She's so rich...and the list goes on. If there were no comparisons and competitions, the world would have been entirely a different place to live.

Simply put, if we compare ourselves with others who have something that we wish we had and feel sad (or angry) about it, we call it jealousy!

We have a bad habit of BIFURCATING everything into GOOD or BAD. But we must understand, most of the aspects in the world are in GREYSCALE, not just BLACK n' WHITE.

Since we have to put jealousy into one of the two buckets, we put it into the BAD bucket. Hold on!! There can be a positive jealousy too. It just depends on what you are jealous of and how you handle it.

You may have observed, we never develop this feeling with anyone far from our level or reach. A newly married girl never feels jealous if a Bollywood couple goes even to Switzerland for their honeymoon. But if her neighbour couple dines out in a nearby restaurant (and sets that as a status photo or DP), it upsets her mood! For a girl, it does not hurt if Katrina looks so gorgeous. But if the girl's classmate has one pimple less than her, she starts feeling sad. With people far above us, we never compare, we never compete.

Let me get back to the title – Positive Jealousy.

Simply put, positive jealousy is doing exactly the opposite to the examples above. One, not feeling sad comparing yourselves with mediocre things and people around you. Two, start comparing and competing with people way above your level, again without feeling sad or angry.

I know, it's easy to write such advice but difficult to follow. But let's think. There are so many things beyond your control. You may want to be tall like Abhishek Bachchan but what to do, life doesn't give you the option to choose Amitabh Bachchan as your father. You could not inherit the blue in your eyes, decorum in your voice, straightness in your hair, dimple on your cheek, rose in your lips from your parents. Those who are born with those features are beautiful, handsome, good-looking.. but what about us?

There are different ways of handling this. One, I don't care because it's not my mistake I'm born with ordinary or sometimes ugly features. Two, I try to grow tall, have an artificial blue lens, lip colour or go to an extent of plastic surgery to match myself with them. Three, I feel jealous and feel sad. You know what's the wisest choice!

On the other hand, positive jealousy is all about comparing and competing ourselves with someone having better than what we have, which they have acquired not by birth or just because others donated to them, but something that they acquired through their hard work, perseverance and intelligence.

What an amazing style Paulo Coelho has in his writing! How could Buddha think something that is so relevant even after so many thousands of years!! How amazing is the thought process of Osho Rajneesh, Sam Harris, Chalam!! What an orator Martin Luther King was! How can someone be so determined as Bhagat Singh! How can anyone earn such huge respect from people in one's lifetime as my father did! These are my jealousies, my positive jealousies, or my inspirations.

Positive jealousy never lets you feel sad or angry. It just amazes you, inspires you and motivates you to get closer to them. When

I know my appearance cannot attract, impress or inspire others, I should focus on my strengths. I should be kinder than I am. I should read more than I do. I should think better than before. My speech should be more interesting and meaningful. My smile may not be attractive, but the words I speak should bring beautiful smiles to others' faces. I know I am not handsome or beautiful. And I also know I am trying to hide them, but with a positive mean.

We can forcibly change ourselves. If a girl wears a natural sea green coloured lens, her eyes may look like Aishwarya's. A simple hair straightener can make your hair the same as the one's you dreamt of. Plastic surgery can bend or straighten, shrink or grow any feature of your body. But in the end, I would say you were good before because.. you were you!

There's nothing wrong with developing jealousy. But all that matters is what factors you are feeling jealous of and how you respond to it and handle it. Lighter is in your hand - you can either light a candle or a cigar. The choice is yours!!

CHAPTER TWO

BEING STRAIGHTFORWARD

You must have heard many people saying "I am very straightforward. I speak my heart. I can't have something inside and speak something else. I can't act. You may feel offended; but this is how I am, straightforward..." and so on.

Observe the tone of their voice while telling this. Most of people feel proud of being straightforward.

Honestly, I don't choose to be straightforward most of the time. That shouldn't make you jump the gun and come to the conclusion that I am not truthful. It's just about being diplomatic. It's easy to be straightforward. But when we evaluate its implications against diplomacy, we understand how costly your straightforwardness can be in your personal and professional lives, especially if you're in a leadership position, either at home or at the workplace.

You may interpret 'straightforwardness' as being truthful, honest and transparent. Well, I agree. On the other hand, since most people take the word 'diplomacy' in a negative sense, I would just like to tell, Diplomacy, simply put – is a way of being subtle, tactful, sensitive & going smoothly. We know bitter guard is good for health. But we prefer eating it cooked – baked or fried. Diplomacy is all about baking or frying your thought before expressing it. But straightforwardness is simply serving it raw.

If you express something like "I don't like the colour combination of the dress you're wearing" without the person asking your opinion, even if he or she is your best friend, that creates a small discomfort or embarrassment for some time. I know, that colour combination might have created irritation in you, but why to respect their choice as long as it doesn't disturb or spoil the work or relationships!!

"I don't like the way you work. You show no interest. You definitely need to improve if you want to survive here" says a boss to his subordinate. Observe how straightforward and how vague his comments are! We understand that the intention is good. But this straightforwardness is; first, loosening the bond with the employee by insulting him; second, there is no specific instructions or guidance on "what" to be improved and what is the expected "way" of working; third, the boss has no idea of why the subordinate shows no interest. No root cause is found.

Does it mean one should never get angry? Should we never expect? Well yes, we have to. But, we should channelize a powerful emotion like anger properly. Don't insult your precious anger by shouting it out. Preserve it. Postpone it and use it creatively. We should set expectations after knowing the capabilities and area of interest/expertise of the person or team. Perhaps you are expecting Usain Bolt to win a golf title.

The ideal way would be respecting the tastes, opinions and feelings of the person in front of you, understanding their perspective, and true reasons for not meeting the deadlines or targets (better, taking proactive steps beforehand to avoid this), explaining your expectations beforehand and motivating, guiding and training to reach such expectations and finally, to polish our expressions.

If you say, 'Who has time for all this?' I would say, 'Then.. settle for mediocre results.'

CHAPTER THREE

DYING AS YOUNG GRANDPA

I had a classmate who would always tell a one-liner story: 'There was a very old aged grandma who died when she was very young.' We would just laugh at it without giving it a deeper thought. Perhaps, even he didn't know what it meant. Maybe the story meant, the grandma never let the child in her die. She was young at heart and mature in thoughts.

I have seen some people who live as if they have promised someone that they would never laugh in their lifetime. They are very serious people. They never act silly. Forget about making jokes, they do not even smile openly when others are laughing out loud at your jokes. They do not speak much. And sometimes, we mistake that way of living as maturity, as a sign of intelligence, as a mark of decency.. so on and so forth. This category of people may think that they would be looked down upon by others if they speak more, if they crack jokes and if they laugh out. If that's the case, robots must be the most respected beings. Like we get 'lateral entry' to some academic courses, these people must have got lateral entry to 'life'. They skip their childhood and directly become grown-ups.

How boring!

On the other hand, I have seen people who over-react, over-thank, over-apologize, over-laugh. In simple, they overact all the time, everywhere. Just lend them your pen for a minute to sign somewhere, they would say 'Oh.. thank you so much, I will never forget your help' - as if you have given them a second life. You just say 'thanks' when they do a small favour. They would say 'You're welcome. It's my pleasure to help you. Always ready to help you etc. as if they were waiting to help you for years. Even if you tell them a poor joke, which has been revolving around the world from the age SMS was born and still revolving in WhatsApp, they would roll on the floor laughing as if that's the joke of their lifetime. Their common-sense clock has stopped running long back, but the body clock has been running uninterruptedly. This mismatch makes them absurd.

How irritating!

I prefer to choose between these 'How boring!' and 'How irritating!' paths.

CHAPTER FOUR

IN THE AIRPORT

It's a place from where many dreams take off. This place makes the world smaller by giving people wings to fly. It never sleeps. It sees people going and people coming without knowing where. There come some birds without fluttering wings from the sky and it sees the same birds swallowing the people, flying high and disappearing in the sky.

It sees many emotions on the faces of people every day. Some are sad, some are tensed, some are confused, some are in a hurry and some seem to have an eternity to spend here. But the place remains neutral; perhaps, when it was newly built, it was also confused to see why people are so different. It's an everyday story; but now, this place shows no emotions, just like the people who work here.

I see different people here.

There is a couple, who must be a little over 70 years, with a boy aged about 6 years. It looks like it's their first journey in the sky. Maybe, they are going overseas to meet their son and daughter-in-law, who have gone there to convert dollars or pounds into rupees or to rename 'living' as 'career'. Even though they have visited the airport many times, the procedures here seem new to them today. They are completely ignorant. The man is inquiring every airport officer about the processes in excellent orthodox English, not realizing that English has changed, just like the people. There is a boy, their grandson, who's just enjoying his ride on the trolley on top of a huge traveling bag. He is innocent. Ignorance is not knowing what should have been known and knowing that it should have been known. Innocence is not knowing both. Ignorance and innocence are traveling together.

There is another family with a large herd of girls. They are busy taking selfies. Their camera phone that blinks its eyes, records their faces in its memory will shortly see them uploading them on Facebook, Instagram, WhatsApp and whatnot. From then the number game begins, how many views, likes and loves? One of the elders in the group asks them to stop posing for the camera or they would miss the flight. When they continue, he even makes a poor childish joke in a warning tone that if they miss the flight, they will have to remain in the airport cleaning the floors. The lady cleaning the floor starts rubbing the mob more strongly against the floor giving a warning stare at him.

There are people who are too casual in their dress. They have come with their shorts, three-fourths, night pants as if they are going to buy a shampoo in the shop just beside their home. On the other hand, there is a group of ladies, on their obvious first visit to the airport, who have come dressed up in grand-looking silk sarees. They have realized that they are the minority, trying to hide the embarrassment but feeling comfortable looking at each other. There is another lady, roaming aimlessly, trying hard to hide the wrinkles on her face beneath the make-up, in the western outfit, bargaining time to make her look young, not realizing the fact that old age has its own beauty.

There are people, looking like commandos roaming in the airport with guns, appointed to safeguard people if any massacre takes place. But, instead of creating a secure feeling, they remind us of terror attacks and add to some people's tension. There are air-hostesses and air stewardesses arriving in their uniforms. Some are in dark red and some others are in dark blue uniforms. The colour of their uniforms contrasts with their complexion, exactly like the smile on their contrasting the state of their mind. They seem to be irritated by the ugly looks and insensitive comments they receive from some people. But they choose to be blind to those looks and deaf to such comments; plastic smiles on their faces continue to cover their emotions.

And lastly, here I am, sitting alone and watching the entire world in the airport, waiting for my bird without fluttering wings to come and take me to the skies of a different world.

CHAPTER FIVE

ALL ABOUT GIVE AND TAKE

Here are some questions for you.

During school days, were you enjoying reading your textbooks as much as you enjoyed reading storybooks?

What do you remember for a long time and what can you recall quickly? Is it the multiplication table of 19? Or the 'Ek-do-teen' song from the movie Tezaab?

What touches your heart more and what remains a sweet memory? Is it your marriage? Or is it your first crush and love?

I'm sure, most of you, if not all, would vote for the second options. Just observe the common elements in all of them – there is no 'give n take' there. We enjoyed reading storybooks and lived the characters because there was no fear of the need for writing about those stories in any exam. We hummed along the original ek-do-teen song and it remained a part of our memory permanently as we never worried about reproducing it when someone asked. Love in you sprouted just because it wanted to sprout; not because you would be accepted and respected by the society if you were in love.

We have converted our working into jobs, learning into schooling, love into marriages, study into project, living into religion, eating into dieting, friendship into partnership, devotion into prayer.. the list goes on.

In some cases, the moment our actions become transactional, they cannot reach the fullest height or achieve the best quality. We read our textbooks with a thought running in our mind that we would be tested on all this in the exam and we should reproduce it well. This anxiety about your performance in the exams and the need for getting good marks for a better future make our textbook reading transactional. Our tricky mind remembers the textbook content as long as the purpose is served. Once the exams are complete, the knowledge we accumulated from textbook starts fading away.

Similarly, it was all good until the man needed a reason for the creation and running of the universe. He called it God. From a common man's perspective, perhaps, it's fair to assume there should be some 'power' controlling nature. Unfortunately, the man didn't stop there. He started transactions with God. "If there is a 'power', why can't we ask it (him) to give us what we want?" – This very question destroyed entire humanity. We started asking God for money, education, courage, health, jobs, visa and worst of all, marriage. But how can God start 'Giving' anything without 'Taking' something from you? (because God is just your brainchild and he thinks and behaves exactly as you do).

Then we started offering fruits, sweets, money, clothes, gold and even liquor. Religions were born, priests were born and scriptures were born. They gave you prescriptions and taught you procedures on how to worship, how to pray, what to offer, when to eat, when to make love and whatnot! We stood, we bent, we rolled, we joined palms, we kneeled down, we shouted, we murmured – we did all that we can – just to 'get' something from God. We believed we should 'give' something to 'get' something without asking a simple question 'If God has CREATED everything (and has authority over it), isn't whatever we give is not ours?'.

We reduced God to the level of a clerk in a government office. Indeed, lower than that, because we steal from his own pocket and bribe him to get your work done. How many of us can worship without asking for anything, either for ourselves or for our loved ones? Transactions keep us mediocre.

Then come love, marriage and relationships. We lowered them to the level of transactions again. Saying 'I love you' to anyone is no fault, but waiting for 'I too' (not me too) is! I love you because I love you, I love the way you speak, think, respond, look, smile, support, console, cheer up, behave and not because I expect these to myself from you. If I expect so, I'm not just loving you. I'm asking you to boost my ego. The moment you seek ego boosting, your mind works like an ego bucket with holes; it never gets filled. We lose the joy of loving because we get busy in filling the bucket with holes.

Marriages and other relationships get down to the business level with a lot of 'give and take'. The core idea of human relationships should be sharing of joys and sorrows. But most of the marriages begin with negotiations on 'give & take' of money and the dirty yellow metal. We have even taken marriage to the next level by making this an ONLINE transaction. We have matrimonial websites where we can shortlist men and women by applying filters like caste, age, profession, height, weight, annual income, colour and so on. The boy has a job in a reputed company – let's 'TAKE' more. The girl is educationally well qualified and working(!) – let's BARGAIN to 'GIVE' less. Where are we heading to? I wish there were filters for the level of 'understanding' and 'love' in the matrimonial websites, which is unlikely to happen.

The greatest education happens when marks are not sought. Newton didn't discover gravitation as a part of his college project. We remember Juliet because she expected no gift from Archies by Romeo (luckily, there wasn't one at that time) and we remember Romeo because he never checked her WhatsApp and call log.

Does it mean we should never set a goal, expect results and work towards achieving them? We should; but not in every aspect. Don't mistake business for passion. Don't call a course entire learning. Don't set success as an endpoint to your effort and keep looking for it. Let your passion continue working until success wakes you up shaking your shoulder.

CHAPTER SIX

FILLING THE BUCKET WITH HOLES

If you have never encountered possessiveness in your life, you're lucky for two reasons. One, you have not undergone that suffering. Two, you don't have to continue reading this article; it's not for you.

Possessiveness is like smoking; it burns both ends. I strongly believe, possessiveness is one of the most undesired byproducts of love. People, who are possessive ask 'How can you love without being possessive?' On the other end, there are people who say 'If you're possessive, you do not love.' It depends on how you look at it; is it through your intellect or through emotions? Well, I have been both - a victim and a culprit - in the matter of possessiveness. And both roles are equally difficult to play.

When someone is possessive about you, I interpret it in different ways: One, you are very important to them. Two, they have a sense of insecurity about losing you. Three, they may have an inferiority complex about themselves. Four, their ego is being hit hard. If you were never possessive about others, you will not feel others' suffering of possessiveness for you. If you're sensitive enough, you know that it hurts and you will start giving them confidence. You will start clarifying their doubts. You will start being transparent. You will make every effort to make them realize they are equally important to you. But possessiveness knows no logic. It's a bucket with holes; you can't fill it. They continue to be possessive about you.

You may be very honest in your efforts. You can honestly see only your partner in your dreams. But you become helpless when your partner starts complaining even when someone else sees you in their dreams! That's how possessiveness progresses. That's the point when you start feeling difficulty answering questions. That's when you feel the suffocation of love. That doesn't mean they doubt your love. It neither means that they think you would get inclined towards others. It's just the unreasonable insecurity that possessiveness brings. You will be tired of convincing, producing proofs and giving explanations. The relationship starts falling apart.

On the other hand, it's even more difficult to handle your possessiveness toward your partner. You know you love them and they love you too. Deep in your mind, you are confident about their love for you. You are a sensitive person. You know you do not doubt their fidelity towards you, but situations make you so helpless and you sound like you doubt them. You want to set them free but you can't. You understand deeply that they have their own space, their own priorities, their interests and their own world. But your heart wants them to make you their entire world. You just don't intrude in their space; you start expecting only you in their times too. Even a many-year-old mundane acquaintance (just a friendship) of your partner starts hurting you. Unnecessary comparisons start! 'Was he better than me?' 'Compared to me, would she be your right partner?', 'Did you like him more than you like me now?' – No, possessiveness doesn't let you sleep.

But wait! Don't jump the gun to conclude you are a sadistic doubting personality! It's just your 'Superego and Id' at fight; your ego is constantly suffering to bridge them. Despite all their efforts, they fail to satisfy your ego. Again, it's a bucket with holes. They get tired of trying to fill it.

We do different experiments in the process of handling possessiveness. When others are possessive about us, there is nothing much we can do other than constantly give them confidence by being transparent. People who are possessive are usually very loving and don't give up easily. But if the person is insensitive, he or she converts his/her possessiveness into sadistic doubting. He or she chooses the easiest route of associating you with another person. It doesn't make sense to hold that relationship anymore. It hurts to depart. But it hurts even more to be in that relationship after love ceases to exist. It's time to say goodbye.

But a more challenging task is handling our own possessives towards our loved ones. To suppress your feeling of possessiveness, you start to associate yourself with someone else – just to show your partner that you have another option too. But that's too stupid and doesn't work. You are not trying to cover the holes in your bucket; instead, you're just trying to pour water from a different pot. Another experiment is 'avoiding your partner and trying to remain yourself'. This doesn't work too. If you avoid it so easily, you wouldn't have loved so deeply.

Next, you start feeling so guilty about your own possessiveness that you decide you would end the relationship. In you, that will start another guilt of going away from someone for none of their mistakes. Then what's the best way to overcome this? Suffer till the validity period of your possessiveness gets over. Suffering possessiveness is the best and the only way I have discovered so far. There are other different options to handle. But none of them seems to work. Give it its time. Possessiveness slowly fades away.

What does the time do? It either gives you so much confidence about yourself and your partner's love towards you that you stop feeling possessive or the time lessens the intensity of your love towards your partner and the possessiveness automatically dies when love is not intense.

CHAPTER SEVEN

A LETTER TO THE DAUGHTER

My dear little girl,

I saw you in the morning standing in the window looking at the sky. I'm sure you were calling rain. Now it's noon and clouds have gathered in the sky. Perhaps rain heard your wish.

If it rains, let's get drenched, smell the petrichor, make paper boats of my old calendars and be happy. But just be prepared, some are just passing clouds, exactly like some people in our life. They don't rain. They just pass by. Don't curse them. They come, give hope, make us dream and pass by. That's the lifespan of the happiness they could give. Be happy. Understand that not every happiness is permanent and something that is momentary can also give us happiness. Happiness is not about taking; it's about making.

Don't be in a hurry. Time runs faster only for elders. They are busy dwelling in their egos, comparing themselves with others, buying what is not needed, then paying EMIs, seeking happiness outside, smiling when they are sad showing the world they are fine, feeling sad for not having even what is unwanted, cursing their jobs, blaming life and giving their children the second-hand dreams and unaccomplished plans. But there is a lot of time for children in life's clock. Go slowly. Grow slowly. I will remain a child as long as you remain the child. I don't want to grow up soon.

One day, unfortunately, you will also grow up and get into a relationship or marry an idiot, just like your mother did. That's okay. Marriage is like a clearance sale. Choose what's least idiotic from the available options. Don't let the world program your mind. Let the world supply the bricks and sand. But it should always be you who should construct the house of your life. Everyone is busy breaking and fixing their own lives. Don't think about how you look to others' eyes. It's only one pair of eyes you should look good to, and they are your own eyes. Don't lend your eyes to others to see their dreams. Don't make your own dreams refugees. Let your eyes see your dreams. Be positively selfish.

The world is not so old to remain black and white. Once it had gods in white and demons in black. Learn to observe and ignore the bad in white and appreciate and apply the good in black. Let's remain humans, choosing to be in grey, a good blend of good and bad. Being positive is not about remaining unaware of the negativity. It's about seeing the unseen good in the negative and remaining blind to the rest of it. True positivity is about being positive about negative too.

Whether you like it or not, you will encounter 'comparisons and competitions' in life as you grow. Learn to handle them well. When you take competitions seriously, it simply means, you want to do something that others are already doing just better than all of them. Instead, believe in CREATING.

Do something that no one else has done. Think in a way that no one else has ever thought. See the unseen. Hear the unheard. Your competition ended when you were a sperm. You raced against millions of other sperms and won the race. You are already created. Now, it's your turn to create. Comparison is an absolute stupidity. You are not a thing to be compared and selected. You are a being.

Let the world compare with others. You just compare your past and your present. Ask yourself 'Have I added value to my life between yesterday and today?' If they answer yes, move on. If no, add value and go ahead.

Be shameless in asking questions. Don't accept without questioning. Most of the times, the world expects you 'just to accept without questioning' and 'just to follow without asking'. It's just because the world either has no answers to your questions, or doesn't want to insult the practices by questioning or doubting our ancestors, or the world is too insecure of questions and changes, or it wants to keep you in dark. Learn to respect the opinions and doubt the ideas. True education is not asking 'Answer the questions' it's about telling 'Question the answers'. Let the world educate you. Get educated yourself as well.

Don't hurt others. But understand the difference between 'You hurting others' and 'Others being hurt'. You hurt when you forcibly make others do that they don't like. They are hurt when you do something that you like to do and others don't like you doing it. You are responsible for the first and don't do it. You are helpless about the second and don't stop it. Set the right expectations about yourself in others. But don't expect others to be right. The definition of 'Being right' differs in each of our dictionaries. But love throws away all these thoughts and rules. It expects. It hurts. When you can't avoid, expect less and get hurt less.

Even after you grow up, don't let the child in you die. It's okay to questions, to be silly, to be funny and to be stupid. Every time you do something different, something that hurts others and creates a disturbance, I always ask you 'Do you think what you did is right?'. You are always honest and say innocently 'No' sometimes and you correct it. By asking that question, I just want to tell you that you are the best judge of yourself. Ask yourself whenever you are in doubt about your decisions and deeds. No one else has the answers except you.

You are a princess though I am not a king. You will remain a princess even if you do not meet a prince. Because being a princess is not relative, it's absolute.

Love,
Dad

CHAPTER EIGHT

FLYING WITHOUT WINGS

Sometimes life becomes devastating overnight. An innocent woman, who never stepped out of home her entire life, loses her loving husband at an early age with young children to take care of. The man, who is the only breadwinner of a poor family, commits suicide leaving behind his wife and children with his old aged parents. Parents get the news of their son securing the first rank in the board exam and the diagnostic report confirming cancer cells in his blood on the same day. A jolly-going girl, the princess in her family gets married to a sadist man and her life takes a U-turn within months with all her sufferings, mental and physical. A middle-aged man who was active, energetic, ever-helping others, independent, suddenly gets paralyzed being unable to lift his own hand. We lose relationships. We lose jobs. We lose money. We lose health. We lose lives. Along with these and more than these, we lose hope and time.

Sometimes the damages are simply the results of our own stupidity. Sometimes the loss is because of others whom we believed. Sometimes the suffering is because of our kindness or innocence. Sometimes, life goes beyond our comprehension and analysis – we call it fate, karma and so on.

For some of the losses, we get the reasons. For some of the sufferings, we get the answers. For some of the problems, we think we could have applied some solution that would have worked. But these are normally not the losses, sufferings or problems that we regularly encounter in life so that we can use all the reasons, answers or solutions to stop them from occurring again. Hence, all the analyses that we make after the damage are just like post-mortem reports. We cannot make the dead one alive. By the time you get ready to share your solution with others, life would stand in front of them giving a different type of problem, suffering and loss. One size doesn't fit all. Sometimes learning lessons is meaningless. Sharing your experience is useless.

What really matters is how you respond to the problem, suffering and loss!

The man who encounters an unexpected loss in business may commit suicide. The girl who expected the first rank may go into chronic depression if she gets the seventh rank. The man who is the victim of the corruption in society may take the gun, enter a forest and become a Naxalite. The boy who is deserted by his girl may seek the shelter of a bar and become an alcoholic. The middle-aged man who is deceived by his wife may go extremely spiritual and become a maniac about god.

What happened to their earlier dreams, their earlier responsibilities, ambitions, happiness and the people around them? Can one disaster change the complete course of their life? Are life's circumstances so powerful that we become so helpless and turn completely into what we were not?

That's when our response to life matters!

The best way to respond to life's disasters is not to respond, at least immediately. Death of dear ones, loss of loved ones, shattering of a dream, and collapse of life's plan – all these definitely hurt a lot. The grief that is caused by all of these has its own validity time. But that's exactly the time that's most negatively tempting too. It tempts you to kill others, it tempts you to commit suicide, it tempts you to cheat others like how others did it to you and it tempts you to feel useless and helpless against life and make you completely handicapped for a lifetime taking away all the confidence from you.

I just stick to the golden words "Let the time pass!"

Remain dead during that time. It's difficult to smile. It's difficult to dust yourself up, stand and get going. It's difficult to get back to work. It's difficult to be as if nothing adverse happened. But it is not impossible as well.

If you forcibly try to deviate yourself or are forced by others to get back to normalcy, it's again a mistake. We are forcibly turning the screw in the wrong thread. It doesn't fit appropriately. Give pain its own time. It should settle down like the sediment at the bottom of the pond when someone throws a stone. We cannot and should not forcibly clear the water. We should wait until the sludge settles down itself.

Slowly the sun rises, clouds scatter and the pain fades away. It's time to call back those incomplete dreams, bring back the left-out relationships and time to start the joy of walking from the first step. It's all new. At least earlier we had the fear of falling down from a great height. But it's a new start. We are at the foot of the hill. Our wings may have been broken by the cruelty of life. But we have dreams, experiences and plans that can take us to the same heights without wings.

One day, after many years, when we sit back and think, we either repent for the hasty wrong step we took after the disaster or we feel proud for letting the time pass and taking the right route.

Let the time pass.

CHAPTER NINE

DEATH NOTE OF SUICIDE

I'm Suicide; death of your own choice. I'm the costliest slave. I can do the last favour for you. I'm the final pain who can stop all the other pains. From the time the human race started thinking, I'm existing in hundreds of forms. I was born to kill. I have just been doing my job; because I am death.

There was a girl who failed in the exam, there was a boy whose love was rejected by a girl, there was a businessman who couldn't repay his loans, there was a young man who was betrayed by his wife, there was a woman who was harassed by her husband, there was an old man whose stomach pain was unbearable, there was an adolescent whose father refused to buy him a bike, there was a man who deserted his wife and children for silly reasons, there was a maniac saint who couldn't find god even after years of search, there was a poor couple who couldn't feed their children every day, there was a millionaire who couldn't face the society after he was caught in an illegal act, there was a mislead young man who sacrificed his life in the name of religion and so on. Everyone had their own reason. I served them all without any discrimination. I do not think about what's right and what's wrong. I just do my job; because I am death.

I am ready to come in any form. Some choose poison – making the deadly substance mix in the blood and run all over the body.

The same blood that travelled thousands of miles within their body through the veins these years and served life, the same blood that they shared with their mother, father, sister and brother, the same blood that connected the entire family now carries poison and welcomes me.

Some choose to hang to death – choking the air that they inhaled from the time they were born; the air that connected humans with the universe by entering in and coming out now stands helplessly at the threshold of their throat, not knowing how to enter into the body and the innocent lungs after waiting for sometimes realize that the man has chosen to embrace me – the death.

Some others choose to burn themselves up – the skin that sensed the loving touch of mother and caring touch of father, the skin that conveyed the desire of the partner and gave security through a hug by the loved one now mercilessly burns in the fire of their anger, helplessness and sadness.

Some jump from heights, some drown in water and some crush their body under the running trains. I had no mercy.

They called me and I killed them. I just did my job; because I am death.

The world doesn't like me. Religions call me a sin. Laws call me a crime. I didn't care. I just wanted to be an honest slave. Whenever anyone decides to embrace me, they become my masters and I become their slave. I obeyed them. They asked me to end their pains by killing them. I did just what they ordered.

People say those who commit suicide are cowards who want to escape from life's hardships. Religions threaten that those who commit suicide will go to hell. Laws have penal codes that declare the punishment of imprisonment for those who attempt to commit suicide. All of these failed to stop me. My masters still called me and I have been killing them for centuries.

No law, no religion and no criticism of the world could stop me. All of them failed because they were utter nonsense and nothing more than jokes.

If someone is a coward, how could he take such a dare step to die knowing that it would be the end of everything?

If laws think they could stop me by punishing those who attempted me, why don't courts understand that people who decide to die aren't bothered about surviving or aftereffects?

If religions think they can stop me by threatening my masters by telling them that they would go to hell, why don't religions understand that the shift from one known hell to another unknown hell doesn't make any difference?

Hence they all failed to stop me. No one addressed the root cause. No one could end me. I have been killing my masters. I have been just doing my job; because I am death.

If there is anyone who can end me, it is no one but I. And I have decided to end myself.

I have decided to end the reason for my birth – killing others. I have decided to stop serving my masters. I just want to tell them 'there is something more and someone else for you'.

Dear student, who are the people to certify your ability by numbers and grades? Not everyone who has achieved and remained unforgettable in the world have big numbers on their marks cards.

Dear young man, be happy your wife betrayed you so early – she is not worth your sadness. Tears are worth and shed them only with dignity. Life is one, don't end it for undeserved people.

Dear businessman, either you should not care about what society thinks about you for being caught in an illegal act or you should answer it in a proper way.

Everyone is busy breaking and fixing their own lives. Society has a short memory. Yesterday's newspapers are today's rags. Fingers that operate the remote controller of the TV are very fickle-minded. They change the news channels once in a few seconds. No one remembers your death. Don't care the society. Just live insensitively. If you care for what society thinks, live – transform yourself and show what you are. Your suicide will either make no difference to society or it will leave a permanent black mark about you.

Dear poor parents, I know the helplessness of not even being able to feed your children hurts. But what rights do you have to kill the innocent when they don't want to die? How can you be so irresponsible to leave them orphans here when you brought them to this world without their request? Don't be so insensitive. Days of hunger will pass. Just search. The world is still green. One day when your child becomes great, they should remember the days of hunger, sow hope and reap life in others' lives.

Dear man, feeling guilty is the first sign of being human. It should be the first step towards correction of your mistakes. Even if it's a mistake beyond correction, then don't you think you deserve punishment by living in guilt? Don't escape punishment. If you are sensitive enough to feel the guilt, you will be sensitive enough to bear the punishment. The world needs sensitive humans like you.

Dear boy, don't end your life just because a girl rejected your love. You are you because of the love shown to you by many. It's time to return. The best way to overcome your pain is to console those who are in pain. Live so well that one day she repents for refusing your love. Success is the best revenge.

I, Suicide am suffering from the same guilt. I had been serving my masters and killing them without thinking about the people around them who were left behind here. Now I see the hardship of the old aged parents who lost their son, I can feel the struggle of an innocent woman who faced society for her children after her husband committed suicide, I can visualize the innocent faces of children who felt the need for their parents every time their friends told about their parents and so on.

I cannot withstand my guilt anymore. My commitment to my job ends here. My honesty towards my masters stops here. My reason for my birth closes here. What's the use of commitment, honesty or purpose of birth when they don't serve any good intentions or lead to happiness! Suicide wants to commit suicide. Everyone who committed suicide for centuries is responsible for my death. Death should be a satisfying phenomenon. Welcome it with a sense of accomplishment. Let the world be happy from now. Goodbye.

10. DEAR REJECTION, SORRY I REJECT YOU...

They got 'married happily' and they remained 'happily married'. The couple had only one wish: having a child. Years passed. They did everything possible. They prayed to multiple gods and confused them, they consulted doctors, got every medical test done, put in their own efforts (Actually the order should have been reversed) and finally, they got the good news they had been waiting for. But after a few weeks; the wife came with a sad face and announced 'miscarriage'! Her body had rejected the fetus from the womb and had thrown it away!

Sometimes rejection starts before birth!

There was a boy, who, despite having all the qualities of a leader, was rejected for contesting in the school leader elections just because he was short.

There was a girl who had extraordinary imagination and great language but our education system rejected her to get promoted to the next class as she could not pass the Math exam.

There was another boy who loved a girl and proposed to her. She rejected the proposal because of fear that her parents would not accept a boy of a different caste.

There was a man who topped every exam throughout his school days. He applied for a job. He got rejected because his English sounded like his mother tongue.

There was a couple who were happy in love life before their marriage. But it's not sure what happened later. Their married life rejected them in the name of incompatibility.

There was a man who got frustrated with his nine-to-five job. He resigned from it and started a business investing all his earnings. The market rejected his business mercilessly. Business toppled upside down.

At school, in exams, in job interviews, in love, in life, in business, in marriages, in other relationships, we keep getting rejected at different stages.

We start many dreams with good hope and with a eat confidence. It takes a lot of time to dream, plan, accumulate confidence, get prepared, start execution and then complete. But all this process gets shattered in a moment. The girl checks her exam results on the internet and it shows 'Failed'. The boy brings months and years of love in his heart and presents it to her. She simply rejects 'I am not interested'. The man comes with a lot of preparation for the interview. At the end of the interview, the interviewer says 'We will get back to you.', which is the company's code to say 'You are rejected'.

Some rejections are beyond our control. How can a boy with excellent leadership skills grow taller overnight to become the school leader? How can the couple teach their chromosomes to be normal to avoid miscarriage? How can the boy, whose love is rejected by the orthodox girl for the difference of their castes, suddenly get re-born in her caste? Impossible!

Some rejections are the results of our own stupidity and lack of the right thought process. We try to leap over a wide-deep trench with overconfidence and fall into it. We don't even make necessary preparations or plans. We try something which is not our cup of tea. We do not identify our strengths, areas of interest and expertise.

We follow some others' advice and blindly believe the one-size-fits-all theory. Just because something has worked great for others does not mean it works for us in the same way as well. Just because your relatives (rivals) or neighbours have admitted their son into the Computer Science branch of engineering and he got selected in the campus interview, you take the same decision for your son. He, who would do miracles, if admitted to a course in fine arts, gets brutally rejected by programming languages and artificial intelligence. A teacher who was best at his profession and who confined himself to classrooms his entire life invests his savings after retirement in a business without knowing and understanding the needs and capacity of the market.

At that moment, it looks like life has come to a halt suddenly!

Most of the times we are so positive that we do not get prepared for hearing a 'No'. We do not keep alternatives ready. We do not ask the questions 'What if..?' and 'What next?'. Being positive does not mean being blind to the undesired results. It simply means to think beyond the negative. It's not about being blindly confident that my road will have no thorns. It's about thinking I won't go unprepared and I go with readiness to encounter thorns and overcome them with the right steps.

Whatever the reasons are, rejections leave us with so many adverse effects. We lose confidence. Fear of failure occupies us. We feel useless and inefficient. It develops self-pity. It makes us think that the world is bad and subsequently that may motivate us to go against our own kindness, honesty, our ethics and goodness. Weak moments that rejection creates make us come to some generic conclusions: the girl who rejects your true love may create hatred in you towards love and all the girls; the exam in which we fail may make us lose trust in the entire education system and exam process; the business attempt that defeats us may make us feel that it is meant only for those who are dishonest. We may start seeking solutions at the wrong places, with wrong relationships through wrong steps just out of anger against what or who rejected us. Rejections may develop a negative viewpoint towards life.

This is exactly when our right thought process can get us out from there. I have found two best ways to fight rejections; One, accept the rejection. Two, reject the rejection.

Let's understand the root cause of the rejection. Could we do anything differently to avoid that rejection? If yes, accept the rejection. Most of the times, life gives a second chance. Go back and try again. Sometimes, life allows you to create a chance. Create it. If it cannot be undone, at least let's accept the fact that rejection is because of our own hastiness and stop blaming life.

If you think, you have done everything at your best and you still got rejected for reasons beyond your control, console yourself. Reject such rejections. Appreciate your efforts. Move on. Just think, you may have invested your kindness, intelligence, efforts, money and time in the wrong person, in the wrong company or relationship, at the wrong place. If yes, try investing it correctly again. Who knows! There may be a girl perfectly meant for you waiting and there may be a course or career that suits your interests, thoughts and skills standing ahead.

Sometimes rejections do miracles and bring fortunes in life! They help you find what you are and what you can be. They close the doors to go to places where others wanted you to go and help you find the doors to reach the destinations meant for you. Years later, you may thank the girl who rejected your love. Had she accepted your proposal that day, you would not have met your soulmate today. You may thank the company that rejected you. Otherwise, you may have not started a company of your own. You may thank the clerk who rejected you in a marriage proposal. That rejection helped you to meet your prince.

Dear rejections, thanks for meeting me now and then in my life. I wouldn't have discovered my strengths without your meets. I accepted you sometimes and I rejected you some other times. You are a part of my life. Let's keep meeting.

CHAPTER ELEVEN

ALL ABOUT EXPECTATIONS

'I didn't expect this from you.' – she said.

'Well, you never told me what you expect.'- He was blunt.

'I thought you would sense what I expect.'

The conversation went on.

*****

If there wasn't something called 'expectation' in this world, there would be no disappointments, no anger, no misunderstanding, no break-up of relationships and so on. At the same time, there would be no successes, no love, no achievements, no inventions and so on. Hence, it's not the expectation that is good or bad by itself; it is just our inability to handle expectations.

In simple words, an expectation is a demand that WE develop on HOW OTHERS should think, respond or act, and WHAT OTHERS should do. Hence the very idea of expectation is prone to pains or disappointments. Here, WE do not have direct control over results because we are not the players but we want OTHERS to do something in the way WE want and give us the result that WE desire. You are not a jockey, but you want the horse to run on the right track and win the race. That's a clear mismatch.

Whenever we expect something from someone, a very common mistake that we do is we forget that the person from whom we are expecting is also an INDIVIDUAL on this planet. He or she has a brain that thinks, a heart that feels and a body that senses. Others may not accept to see from our eyes for they have their own pair of eyes to see.

A father wants his son to study something that he studied and became successful. A mother wants her daughter to become someone that she dreamt of becoming but couldn't. A boss wants his subordinate to think and execute tasks as he does. A boy who expresses his love for a girl wants to hear 'I too' from her. A woman who blindly performs the hardest rituals wants god to answer her prayers and grant her wishes. Nothing wrong in wanting, but it doesn't work that way.

So, SHOULD WE STOP expecting? No, the question should be 'CAN WE STOP' expecting? I haven't seen anyone with minimum intelligence without expectations. Unfortunately, all of us have that element called 'intelligence' in us. But it's all about mending the intelligence to work FOR us; not AGAINST us.

When we know we cannot live without expecting from others, it is always wise to prepare others to meet our expectations, without hurting them. Parents never speak to their son or daughter on their expectations about getting them married to someone belonging to the same caste, religion, financial status and so on. One day, suddenly they get shocked or disappointed when they hear that their children loved or married someone different than what they expected. The children also get shocked to know that their parents' did not accept this.

Not everything can be sensed or understood unless they are expressed and explained. Isn't to wise to SET expectations from the beginning to avoid these shocks and disappointments in life. Almost the same happens with children's studies, career and so on.

It's not about being right or wrong; it's about being wise and minimizing miseries in life.

This is one side of the story. How about the others who CREATE expectations?

It's not always the fault of those who expect. It's also the fault of those who create expectations.

Without our knowledge, we sometimes create expectations in others. The children who are very obedient CREATE expectations in parents that they would listen to everything from their parents. The girl or the woman who treats her man above god creates a false impression that she can sacrifice her life for him. The boy or the man who shows so much love and care at the beginning makes his partner think he has no other world to deal with. The employee who shows high dedication and enthusiasm at work makes his boss rely completely on him or her.

But they all forget: interests change, dedication fades, the ego develops, a 'taken for granted' attitude arises, boredom builds up and the same child, the same girl, the same man, the same employee starts looking different. Of course, they might have not told explicitly that they would be obedient, loyal, caring, loving, super-performing and so on for their entire lifetime. But they definitely CREATED expectations through their words and actions. And when all those start diminishing, the other side starts getting disappointed.

Not everything is expressed or explained verbally; a few matters are just sensed and (mis)understood by the other end. One may argue that 'I did not CREATE expectations. They just developed it themselves.' But the damage is damage. It hurts. Isn't it wise not to create expectations when they cannot be fulfilled until the end?

Expectations are neither good nor bad by themselves. We just fail to SET expectations for those whom we want to be as we wish and we fail to stop CREATING expectations for those that we cannot fulfill.

There is a NOBLE side of EXPECTATIONS; setting expectations for YOURSELF. I expect myself to be more sensible, more sensitive and kinder. This way, if I fulfill my expectations, I am happy and a better human being. If I can't meet my expectations, I have no one else to blame but myself. And I'm sure we all love ourselves so much that we cannot easily blame ourselves.

Finally, should we stop expecting?

Well, that's safe and you can avoid pains.

So, should we expect?

Well, it gives immense happiness when expectations are fulfilled and it depresses you when they are not.

Tough choice.

CHAPTER TWELVE

POOR PAHOM EXISTS IN ALL OF US

I remember a short story titled 'How Much Land Does a Man Need?' written by a great Russian writer - Leo Tolstoy. Quoting from my memory here's a real quick summary of that:

Once a man named Pahom develops greed for lands. He wants to buy more and more land and earn more. He comes across Bashkirs (Turkic people) who own really a huge amount of land. They present an unusual offer. Pahom is offered just to pay 1000 rubles and get as much land as he wants. All he needs to do is to just start walking (or running) from a starting point when the sun rises and return to the same point before the sun sets. He can walk as far as he can and get all the land he walked through. IF he doesn't reach the starting point at the time of sunset, he neither gets any land nor the money he paid. Pahom feels excited, pays 1000 rubles and starts walking. With the greed to get as much land as he can, he walks so long-distance and gets so exhausted that he falls down and dies at the starting point. At last, the Bashkirs bury the body in a six-by-three land justifying the title of the story.

At the surface, the story may just look spiritual trying to advocate us just to come out of our materialistic love for worldly matters; just to be content with what is needed. But for me, it opens different windows.

We walk in the land of relationships like Pahom!

The couple who comes to know about the complications during the delivery of the baby just prays for a safer delivery without losing the lives of the mother and the baby. When the delivery is successful but the baby has some disorder, they get upset thinking that the baby should have been healthy comparing it with the one in the next bed of the maternity ward. As the child grows, fights the disorder and becomes healthy, the parents look at his marks card and wish he had some more marks. Then some more responsibility, then some better offers in the campus interviews, some better salary, then some better company onsite assignment.. the expectations keep expanding. The Pahon runs farther and farther.

This seems to happen in every relationship. Pahom seems to exist in most of us. He does not know how far to run, where to stop and when to return. More than these, he only knows what he wants; not how much he wants. It's all about understanding that there are limitations to everything and to everyone. We just fail to see them. Although the land of love is infinite, the time of the relationship is limited. We should understand where to stop! We forget to take rest. We forget to give rest. We spend all our energy and we exhaust others around us as well.

The boy who just wished for one smile from the girl at the beginning goes to an extent of questioning and doubting her for casually smiling at others. The man who just starts his business for livelihood starts thinking of starting another business as soon as he accumulates some money. A middle-class man who is tired of paying rent wants to build a house for shelter. But soon he starts dreaming of some more houses as assets for his children. Is it wrong to dream? To progress? No, but it's important that you remember the purpose, give yourself time and health to enjoy what you wished for and more importantly, remember that you may be following some incorrect route or harming others in your journey. Pahom should remember his purpose, stop at the right point, take a break and move back.

Another disease that systematically kills our life and our relationship is 'diminishing interest'.

The mind asks itself "I have got what I wanted. What next?" – the question is fine for intellectual aspects like your studies, a position in your workplace, an achievement in your field, or a dream in your life. But how about emotional aspects?

I have got a good friend. I have got a good partner. I have got my soul mate – the question cannot be 'What next?'. It should be 'why next?'

But that's not easy. Our mind fails to differentiate between intelligence and emotions; things and people. We tend to get bored of what we have, we tend to seek something new unnecessarily; we tend to get attracted to something not explored before; we tend to 'take for granted' – although it's named 'seven-year itch', it may happen much before.

Someone with whom you were waiting to spend time, if available freely for a longer time, gradually becomes boring. The person whom you admired from a distance will become ordinary if you get his or her intimacy. Only the tourists exclaim 'Wow!' when they see the Taj Mahal for the first time.

The photographers or the guides who see it every day have no such fascination towards it.

The girl who looked very beautiful as a girlfriend becomes an ordinary wife, the boy who sounded very different as a lover becomes 'just like any other' husband, the teacher who was very interesting when he took the first class becomes very boring as the days pass.

Your friends, your colleagues, your neighbours – everyone undergoes this 'diminishing interest' phase. Do they really change and become boring? Well, the answer is: partially yes and partially no.

They do not change completely. But in our eyes, their company becomes old. The repetition creates boredom. On the other hand, they do not present the best of themselves to you as the days pass. They feel the same about your company. It's old. It's already been achieved. It's taken for granted. The interest that a salesman or a salesgirl shows when you go to buy something new, the way they present is obviously not the same if you go the next day to exchange the item you purchased the previous day because of some damage, defect or dislike. Yesterday, it had to be sold. Today, it is sold.

The other way could be: after we have achieved a relationship, we are confident of its bonding and may feel it's not necessary to nurture it with immense care. It survives itself; just a confidence of being understood.

But growing expectations and diminishing interests – both kill a relationship, gradually. Should we stop being killed? If love still exists, yes!

When the expectations grow beyond a limit, we hug the loved one so tightly that they feel suffocated, so breathless that they want to come out of the hug. When the interest is diminishing, the hand of the loved one is so loosely held that he or she can easily get detached.

So, it's all about loosening the hug and tightening the holding of the hand. The first one gives them breathing space to be comfortable with you and the second one stops them from forgetting your role and importance in their life.

Pahom should know where to stop and when to return. Continuous running exhausts him and he may not return to the point he wanted to arrive at. Running for a very short distance and arriving back early gives him comfort but leaves him with lesser land.

It's important that we give the right and get the best.

CHAPTER THIRTEEN

THE GOD RESIGNS...

I am God.

Usually, people resign from their jobs for one of two reasons: one, when they do not get what they expect and deserve; two, when they see a pasture on the other side of the hill, which they think is greener than the present one. But I am God; I'm resigning for exactly the opposite reasons: one, I have got more than I deserve. Two, my departure from your pasture will make it greener than it presently is.

I am resigning from the job that I never did and from the position I never held. It was you who invented, explored, expected, exploited, exaggerated – everything about me. I am now exhausted. I kept ignoring you for centuries and millennia; you kept making your lives complicated in my name. Now it's high time that I openly submit my resignation and express my disassociation from you.

You decided what's my colour, my name, shape, size, likes, dislikes, character – I just thought you may want me to be like you to feel a better bonding. You wrote stories about me: you made me a creator, protector, saviour, judge, punishing authority, manager, destroyer – I tried to see your creativity in that and understood that you need a support system to answer all your unanswerable questions. You built temples, mosques, churches, chanted my names, hummed hymns, sang songs praising me – all was okay as I thought you need a place and some practices to get peace of mind, some words for achieving concentration and ways to forget your own problems and pains. But things started falling apart.

Your creativity went absurd; you depicted me as a drunkard, a murderer, a rapist, a cheater – someone having all the weaknesses and limitations you humans have; sometimes worse than the darker side of you. How do you expect a god with all these bad qualities to do anything good to you? But you still continued worshipping me without questioning those stories. You made mistakes, blunders, crimes, sins and offered me perks to forgive you and to grant permission to do the new ones.

You offered me money, clothes, food, and weirdest of all, your hair! If you truly thought I was the creator of this Universe, how could you think I need those coloured currency notes, those metal pieces, food and hair from you! You offered me all these for fulfilling your wishes – you need money, you need health, wealth, education, popularity, power, position, visa, funniest of all - marriage! To get your work done you offered me the cheapest of perks – you brought me down to the level of a government office clerk, a travel agent, or a broker.

Well, I just ignored looking at your stupidity. But your stupidity started turning into harmful intelligence. Your illogical religions evolved, your incompetent scriptures got created, your prophets, popes, swamis, gurus, mullahs, priests – all were born in my name. You created a logically absurd, mentally retarded, ethically backward world for yourself.

They explained that you need me, the god, to keep society in order, to keep the fear of someone who can punish the bad and reward the good. They explained that what you do is being counted and you will go to hell or heaven afterlife. They created a 'judgment day', 'Jannat, 'hell'.. what not!

All these attempts were made to suppress your common sense, your reasoning and your ability to think and question. How many centuries can anyone be made to believe? Isn't love, logic and truth the correct ways of living? Why couldn't any religion teach that you should be good and kind not because of fear that some power will punish you if you aren't, but just because you are a human? Why couldn't so-called religious leaders inspire you to be good without creating a need for some reward or lure like heaven?

You systematically killed humanity in my name. You wanted magic, myths and miracles – you never wanted someone who can tell you to work hard, work honestly, not to cheat others; instead, you want to follow someone who can walk on water, who can hear an unspoken voice, who can bring ashes and black marble from nowhere.

You did a crime by creating my forms, my idols, by building temples, mosques and churches and you continued fighting for supremacy. You wanted to expand the number of followers for me, you wanted your religions to grow. You wanted me to act exactly as your kings and politicians. You forgot you should share the same land; you fought, you destroyed and you killed and got killed.

Some people declared themselves as my agents. They acted as messengers between me and you. They started exploiting others, created fears, suppressed questioning, gave solutions for your problems that benefitted them – all in my name. They never constructed roads or bridges, they never invented machines, they never sowed the seeds and reaped the grains – they simply sat in their religious centres their whole life preaching stupidity to people, misleading them, acting as parasites and scavengers – what a waste of human resource!

I know that your devotion towards me is not pure. You just think that you believe me; that's not true. When you suffer from a deadly disease, I have never seen any of you enclosing yourself in a temple or mosque or church, chanting my name, humming my hymns, praying me to cure your diseases without going to any doctor. You justified this by giving the excerpts of your own stupid religions that taught you: you should do your work and pray to god. Only then God will protect you. You never decided: If I have to do my work, let me do it completely and take ownership of my success or failure. You forgot that your kindness and intelligence are the best support systems.

It's now time for me to tell you 'I quit.' It's your world, your life. To be correct, do not expect someone sitting up to watch you and punish you if you do something wrong. Attain maturity and manage yourselves. You're humans: create a heaven yourselves here when you're alive by being good. I have already complicated your lives. I have already become the reason for your stupidity, suffering and incorrect solutions. You have got brains; think. You've got hearts; feel. You've got wings; fly.

CHAPTER FOURTEEN

A Life Skill Called Acceptance

Wrong mix!

It happens most of the time. Life sells some unwanted, unexpected and undesired add-on products in the package. When we need just money from the job, it comes with stress. When we want just the joy of being loved, it brings some pains. The happiness of success demands sacrifice and hard work beforehand. Tasty junk foods come with the threat of spoiling health. The convenience that modern technology brings comes with so many dangers. While a child (and grown-ups who still have a child awake in them) is getting the joy of playing in soil and rain, the elders warn 'Don't play. You will catch a cold, infection..' and so on.

Are life, nature and the system we have built around so sadistic? Why don't they just sell what we want to buy? Just painless love, just stress-free money, easy success, healthy and tasty junk food, no side-effect technology and so on. Why don't we get just what we want!?

We get so many metaphysical, hypothetical and consoling answers and solutions. Some suggest that we ignore the undesired elements and take only the good part of them like the myth that the geese just drink milk and leave the water. Some others suggest that we must face everything we get. Does that really make even the undesired, unwanted products pleasant? No way. They may just divert us; but not completely nullify the stress, pain, ill-health and hard work.

We cannot expect the sun to emit only light that helps us see and not the hot rays that create sweat and irritation! Heat and light come in a package.

Ignoring is not always easy. Facing or fighting is sometimes hard. The nobler way is to accept and experience. The same question arises. Does it nullify the pain, stress or unpleasantness? No, it won't but acceptance makes it tolerable. It prepares us to pass through the phase smoothly when ignoring or facing are not the options.

Parents' and grandparents' beliefs, practices and ideas sound obsolete, irrelevant and out of fashion. We call it the generation gap. But is labeling enough? How to fill the gap? Can we 'accept' at least whatever is possible? because even they had felt and accepted something odd and unnatural about us. There was a misunderstanding and two friends stopped speaking with each other because of some difference in opinions. We don't have to accept their opinions. But are we mature enough to accept and continue the friendship? When the person whom you love and trust so much gives you pain for some reason and If you can accept the person, the relationship is saved. If you at least accept the pain, the life is saved.

Acceptance is preparing ourselves to take things and handle them smoothly. It's far better than ending ourselves up in bars, drowning in depression, creating friction, playing the blame game, or losing someone or something permanently for temporary reasons.

Pure acceptance doesn't mean compromising. The very idea of compromise means accepting unwillingly. Anything that is done unwillingly neither gives happiness nor leads to success or the desired outcome. And no compromise can survive for a long time. You cannot wear a mask and act untrue of yourself forever. It suffocates you. You will fall apart soon. Hence, acceptance is a whole process of feeling the importance of something and someone, dropping our ego and allowing others' words, feelings, wishes and happiness to sink deeply into yours. It needs a calm mind, deeper introspection, and maturity.

Does it mean we should accept something even if it is immoral? Something that forces us to go against our character, our value system and our beliefs? Well, we just need to be open enough to think that such 'acceptance' may also enrich and contribute to our character and value system.

Isn't it fair to accept some pain from those who love us unconditionally? Isn't it okay to accept some anger from those who care for us so much? Isn't it sensible to allow them to exercise some rights on us when they took our responsibilities for so long? In relationships, it is not about who is right or what is right, it is about what is important.

When something is beyond ignoring, beyond facing and beyond acceptance. The only way is to end it, if possible. But before ending, let's try the other options. And let's try them honestly.

CHAPTER FIFTEEN

The Game of Drawing and Erasing Lines

'Mind your own business' – he drew a line curtly.

'Scold me; but don't be sad or silent.' – she erased a line softly.

We express our emotions in different ways with different intensities; sometimes we are subtle and sometimes harsh. If we observe carefully, except for the basic communication needed for interactions with others in daily life, we are constantly drawing our image in others' minds.

He is an angry bird. The florist lady is so motherly. The bus conductor is so funny. That neighbour is very irritating. Her husband is a moody fellow. My friend's wife will sell him one day... and so on. We draw our opinion based on our observations and interactions. More than this, they draw their image on the canvas of our minds.

Then starts our next step: without our knowledge, we start drawing or erasing lines.

Every word, every smile, every gesture, every facial expression, every touch, every tear, every message, every silence, every negligence keeps doing the work of drawing or erasing the lines between you and the others in the background.

A nasty boy follows a college-going girl and makes weird attempts to get close to her everywhere. She chooses to draw a line by showing her footwear, by accompanying her brother or father or even by warning directly based on how diplomatic, daring and irritated she is. A lady offers a seat beside her in the bus to a man who was just a colleague to indicate she is erasing the line to get promoted from just a colleague to a 'would-be' partner. After a regular fight and no talk for some time or days between the couple, the husband prepares a cup of coffee and offers it to the wife. Some other lady, after trying all possible ways to adjust and live together, decides to depart and sends a divorce notice to her husband. The man who promised to help a boy in getting a job gradually gets irritated with the latter's continuous calls, avoids receiving, starts receiving and finally blocks the contact.

Most of the time, we draw or erase lines indirectly. Unless we are insensitive we do not force the other person to erase the line for us and we do not draw the line rudely. The true problem occurs when one wants to keep the line and the other wants to erase it. They are one-sided relationships. They are not necessarily a girl and a boy in love. They can be two friends after a misunderstanding, a married couple after severe differences, colleagues with ego clashes, brothers with family fights and so on. Some lines are erasable but some lines remain permanent. In such cases, it's always sensible to accept the truth and let the line remain drawn. There's no use of post-mortem. It anyway cannot make the dead man alive. If we think post-mortem helps us to handle other relationships better in the future by avoiding the same mistake, it's just our illusion. Life comes up with a new question paper every time.

Erasing the line too early and letting others come close to you may create some possible problems or disappointments: one, you will gradually start realizing what you thought isn't what it is; two, they may start taking you for granted, start taking advantage of you; three, it becomes very difficult for you to draw the line again.

There is a more sensible way of avoiding such mismatch: take time.

Many a time we are hasty in erasing lines. We let people enter into our inner orbits too fast. We do not take time to understand their ideas, thoughts, maturity, tastes, attitude, temperament, the value they show towards relationships, their lifestyle and so on.

We just love the change. We love the newness. We just see what we want to see; not what they are. We do not give them the time to decide whether they are compatible with us. It's not about long-term relationships like marriages; it's important to take time even for other relationships, except the 'on-the-go' interactions at shops, travels and so on.

The same happens with drawing lines also. Every relationship comes with a line with a certain thickness at the beginning. We get introduced, acquainted, understood and bonded in the course of time.

That's when the thickness of the line gets reduced. But if something adverse happens, we try to draw the line again. How we draw the line again matters. Before that, it's important to think if it is really necessary to draw the line again. If it's truly inevitable, it's sensitive to make sure we make it as less painful as possible to both —ourselves and the person on the other side of the line.

The line was not erased from one side. Both of us had erased the line and created that bonding. Now, if only you want to draw the line again, it's human to make it less painful irrespective of who contributed to the collapse of the relationship.

The ideal way of doing the circus of drawing and erasing the lines is to achieve a perfect handshake between your logic and emotions. We miss the happiness that relationships bring if we are too precautious and keep the line intact with everyone.

At the same time, we lose control of our own value and give control of our emotional well-being to others if we carelessly erase the lines. The game of drawing and erasing lines must go on but only after taking time, knowing when, with whom, how and how much!

CHAPTER SIXTEEN

THE WISE DON'T ADVISE

You can see plenty of such people around you. They are experts in every matter. They are walking Google and talking Wikipedia. There's no statement called 'I don't know' in their life. They can talk about anything under the sky and advise anyone in the world.

Here are some samples:

Trump wasn't elected for the second time because of his favouritism too much towards the business sector. You know you don't need any special treatment for cancer; just chew neem leaves every morning for 6 months and see the results. I challenge any type of cancer at any stage.

They are geniuses!

It doesn't need a long time or effort to prove that they are not authentic about the information they give. Just ask them: what is the source of their information? any authentic book? website? words of any expert in the field? any survey? any live example around them? No, they just present some vague baseless illogical information with absolutely zero research.

There are others who show their expertise in every field through their comments or feedback.

Kohli made a mistake; he must have played cover drive a little late. A R Rahman should change the way he composes his music. There is no newness. It's all monotonous now. To reduce the price of essential goods, the Prime Minister should stop exporting those necessary items to other countries and focus first on fulfilling our needs. The advising goes on.

Such people wouldn't have held a cricket bat in their lifetime. They wouldn't have touched the keyboard with their fingertips too. They wouldn't even know if the goods they are speaking about are really exported. But they comment without thinking about what they speak.

Some others still go one step ahead and advise on others' personal matters.

Mechanical Engineering is the evergreen branch; just don't think anymore and just tell your son to choose that branch. Are you not thinking about your daughter's marriage? It's already late. Start searching and get her married soon. I tell you: stop taking any English medicine right from today and do yoga and your diabetes runs away in two months completely.

Ask them: Have you done the same Mechanical Engineering course and achieved something great in life? No. Do you know what the boy is interested in? No. Do you know if the girl or at least if her parents are interested in getting her married? No. Do you know their plans, expectations, financial status and so on? No. Have you stopped taking any medicine immediately and started controlling blood sugar levels in your body by just doing yoga even when it was exceeding 400 mg/dL? No.

They throw advice just because it is someone else's life.

Does it mean we should never give or seek advice? Should we always research and be subject experts before commenting or criticizing? Should we not interfere in other's life? Well, the answer is almost Yes.

We tend to lose our value when we advise without it being sought. Unsought advice is like an unwanted pregnancy. Either the advice will be aborted or the advisor himself, or both.

When we speak about something serious, if not the subject expertise, at least we need some necessary knowledge and basic research. Remember that either the listener is sharp enough to understand that we do not have the content if we speak vaguely or we are just misleading a person who believes that we know about what we are speaking. The first one brings our level down and the second one is a sin.

Even if someone seeks advice on something we are not fully confident about, an honest 'I don't know' or 'I'll find out and get back' helps much. Let's not try to be a guru pretending we have answers and solutions for everything.

Sometimes our advising habit is an effort to overcome our inferiority complex. When we know deep inside that we are experts in any subject or we are not special in any way so that others can identify and appreciate us, we tend to fight that feeling by advising or speaking something baseless. It's the trick of your mind to keep your ego saturation level stable. Otherwise, we may feel useless about ourselves and go depressed.

Sometimes it's our superiority complex on ourselves and underestimation of the person in front of us that makes us give advice. When someone thinks he knows everything, he loses the ability to think about others' knowledge and expertise.

Most of the time, it's our insensitiveness that makes us advisors. If we are insensitive we don't care whether the other person is interested in receiving our advice. We start advising even if not asked for. Worst of all: we advise without standing in their boots. Before advising, we forget to ask ourselves: if we were in such a situation, facing such a problem, would we implement the advice that we are about to give? Or am I just giving a piece of advice just because it's not my problem and not my life?

It's not always the fault of such advisors; sometimes it's also the fault of the seekers. We sometimes seek the advice of the carpenters to advise us on the best car to purchase. We approach the wrong people. We do that out of the trust, love, or respect we have for the person. But we forget to draw a connection between what we want to get and who is right to help us get what we want. This is how a person who made a great career as a religious guru after dropping out of high school for getting single-digit marks in every subject advises you on the career options for your children.

Not every piece of advice is vague and useless. It just depends on whom we approach, who gives and how we receive it. Some advise us purely out of care: drink sufficient water, reach home before dark, don't talk to strangers, don't wear these kinds of dresses, don't skip food – the list goes on. Here, it's simply the care! It's not about our ignorance or inability about managing ourselves. Even the person who tells all these knows that you know these. But love is a sweet stupidity. It's foolish to analyze such advice, idiotic to get irritated with them, insensitive to tell them not to advise because you have grown up and are now self-managed. We should simply listen, smile and move on.

In the end, I want to give three bits of advice, just three: One, learn to advise only when sought by others and seek advice only when needed, with the right people. Two, neither be too arrogant not to take any advice from anyone nor be too weak to take every advice from everyone. Three, learn to ignore the advice that comes from various people on the way if you feel they are unwanted, including all these three bits of advice.

Usually: the wise don't advise.

CHAPTER SEVENTEEN

The Wing That Makes Flying Difficult

I call it WING - the 'World Is Not Good' view.

We often see people speaking or expressing their ideas through general talks, social media and so on. One category of such expressions is about self-pity, blame game and the 'World is not good' attitude.

Some forwarded messages, some people's talks and some stories (?) & status in social media go like this:

'Don't believe anyone; even your own shadow leaves you at night', 'Don't be kind. It costs you a lot', 'The world is good for those who are cunning. It is crooked for those who are kind', 'this world is not for me and I am not for this world' and so on.

These quotes and words are catchy. We somehow feel it is our feeling too. We connect ourselves with it. This happens just because our tricky mind always wants us to be in the good books. There's nothing wrong with it; but the danger starts when we start thinking that the 'World is not good', which is completely not true.

We find some strange happiness in thinking (or believing) that we are good but something bad happened to us; we did everything but we have still suffered; we are honest but we are still cheated. It may be true that you are good, you had done everything and you are honest. But the second parts of the above statements need a different approach to understand.

One: life does not operate on the 'give good and get good' formula. It may discourage us from doing good and falsify the 'karma' theory but that's the way we should understand it.

We should simply be good and do good even after knowing (or expecting) that something good may not come in return. The moment you do good and wait for the good things to return, if (or when) something adverse happens to you, you start blaming life that it did bad to you even after being good. That collapses your happiness.

At least if you could disconnect the bad that happened from the good you did, and think that both of them are independent phenomena, you could focus more on solving or handling the bad in a better way than blaming the world, life and feeling that the good things that you did went in vain. That discourages you from being and doing something good again. And WhatsApp, Facebook status, forwarded messages and philosophies start to attract us.

Two: the more you focus on the bad things that happened to you, the more you lose the ability and focus to look at so many other good things that are available around you and the good people around you. Sometimes we suffer not fully because we have problems that happened to us, but simply because when we suffer we fail to look at the solutions and good things and people around us. Shifting of focus is difficult but it's important.

Three: When we are suffering, when we encounter a failure, when we feel cheated, when in pain or rejected, we seek reasons, not solutions. Well, that's not the time to find the reasons because self-pity is at work at that time. When you are already in pain, your mind does not want to make the situation still worse by telling the truth that you are (or you are also) the reason for your failure, suffering or rejection. It tries to boost your ego with a positive lie that you are all good; the mistake is by others. That's when the self-pity and blame game start. That's when the 'WING' starts developing and you fly in the wrong way.

Is it wrong to console ourselves even with such lies? Well, it just makes you believe there is no good in the world except you and that shuts the doors of hope and happiness.

Just give suffering, problem or rejection their own time to settle. Just recall all the good things that happened to you till now. Just remember all the good people who helped you, sowed hope in you and stood by you in tough times. Let's not generalize that the 'World Is Not Good'.

Life's like operating a modern-day camera. There's a subject and there's a background. Tap on what you want to see clearly and what you want to appear blurry. Keep the people who cause pain in the background and make them blur. Your happiness should be your subject - keep it in the foreground - clear and sharp. One day when we get spaceships to Saturn and jets to Jupiter, we can go there blaming this word. Until then, just focus on the goodness and happiness around you in this world!

CHAPTER EIGHTEEN

GIVING THE JOY OF GIVING

The English student in me is an insomniac; he never sleeps. The more I try to know and think, the more I understand my limitations. By the time I get clarity on one confusion, another confusion queues up itself. I enjoy my limitations and confusions. Thank God! I don't know everything. Perhaps that's the best way to learn.

Here are some words: get, take, grab, earn, snatch, and so on. Although these words indicate the same results, they differ in how they happen: whether they happen with love, through force, with dignity, with rudeness or out of sympathy. Similarly, there are their counterparts: give, donate, throw etcetera.

Which of these actions make you happy?

There were days in my childhood when the greatest reward and the most affordable luxury I could get was going with my father and having a masala dosa (a South Indian dish) at Gayatri Bhavan, one of the decent hotels in the town. Sometimes when I scored good marks in the tests, sometimes when I was sad or upset, sometimes when my father would sense that I was reluctant to eat what was cooked at home, and sometimes for no reason, my father would take me to Gayathri Bhavan, order a masala dosa and sit in front me, enjoying seeing me eating it bite by bite. Though I hadn't asked anytime, I always wondered, why would my father not order one for himself too. I now realize that he was getting the 'joy of giving', just giving.

I have sensed the same with my mother. She never feels hungry when there's only little food left at night. Like anger, giving and sacrifice are the other beautiful ways of expressing your love.

Some people grow beyond their role in our life. A sister takes the role of the father and strives to set right her brother's life, a friend stands like a brother in the toughest times of life, a boss becomes a sister and guides and helps in every walk – Why do they do all this? Is it a way of expressing their gratitude to us? Do they expect us to return it later? No way. Giving gives them happiness. It's absolutely stupid to ask why they do all this. It's sheer love, nothing else.

They don't have to be very big. The bill paid at a hotel for one-by-two cup of coffee two friends have, the favourite food that someone who loves you brings for you, some money kept in your pocket by your brother when you're travelling to a different place, the favourite chocolate that you give to your little girl irrespective of how old she is to the world, a pen gifted by your students spending the pocket money their parents had given them, some sweets brought by a sister feeling that her brother is still a small boy although he's grown up and can get and afford that easily – the list goes on. These are just the acts of expressing love. Just give them the joy of giving.

Although it is rude to reject gifts, sometimes it hurts to know that it costs them a lot to 'give' something to us. Sometimes, in the process of making us happy, they may spend months of their earnings and days of their sacrifice. Hence it is important to be a sensible giver. How can we think that someone who loves us can receive anything happily if we have to suffer or sacrifice to give them something! When there's love, it doesn't matter how big or how costly our gift is.

Sometimes giving may give joy to the giver, but it will be a pain to receive. A father who wants his son to study some course may have the best intention of 'giving a great career' to his son. A mother who wants her daughter to get married to her relative may be thinking that she's 'giving the happiest life' to her daughter, but again, in the rush to give the best to their children, they forget to think if that makes their children happy. Joy in giving should create joy in receiving too.

On the other hand, we snatch the happiness of loved ones from the joy of giving for our own silly reasons. I have seen some people setting a principle for themselves: I don't give or receive gifts. Love is abstract; but not the ways of expressing it. There's no cardiogram invented so far that can convey how much your heart loves someone. It's done most of the times by 'giving' and 'receiving'. For some people, their ego stops them from receiving from others. Ego and love never mix. Some people refuse to receive just because it's a burden for others to give. Well, refusing doesn't serve anything except hurting them. Isn't it sensible to explain that you would be happier to receive small things than to receive such costlier ones beyond their affordability? Sometimes we stop our children from receiving from others in the name of manners, including receiving from their grandparents. Let's not snatch such happiness from giving.

On a lighter note, there are some other people who DEMAND your GIVING: Wish them a Happy birthday and a Happy Wedding Anniversary.

CHAPTER NINETEEN

LIFE LESSONS BY ZERO

A little girl, who was about to get married in a couple of months came for a walk with a man named 'No One'. He was her guide, friend, father, child - he had played many roles. So, he was 'No One'.

Breaking the silence, walking on the seashore, the little girl asked "Teach me something this evening."

He smiled at her as though he knew she read his mind. He started:

"Be a Zero. I'll teach you five lessons that Zero has taught me."

Be a good company!

When Zero comes on the right-hand side of any number, it increases the value of the number ten times. Add such value to the life of whoever comes into your contact. They should feel proud of having you with them.

Don't change others; accept them as they are!

When standing on the left side, added or subtracted, Zero doesn't make any changes to any numbers. Sometimes it's important to accompany others without making your influence on them, nor expecting them to change.

Be tough when needed!

When multiplied by any number, Zero has the power to make them zero too. Sometimes it's important to make others realize that you're powerful. It's a mistake to raise your voice unnecessarily. It's a sin to keep calm when others make the mistake of raising their voice.

Remain humble!

Zero can add value to others, but another number is needed for Zero to show that it can add value. Know the fact that you are nothing by yourself even if you can add great strength to others. Co-living is not a choice.

Remain unique. Act differently!

While all others numbers decrease the value of others when they divide, Zero raises the value to INFINITY when any number is divided by it. Don't divide others. Elevate the relationships!

The sun was slowly sinking at the other side of the sea.

'No one, let me walk on your right side now' - said the little girl.

'You're always right.' - said No One.

The setting sun smiled promising them that he would return again.

CHAPTER TWENTY

THE LOVELIEST REVENGE

"In revenge, most of the time, WE pay the fee for teaching a lesson to OTHERS", I said metaphorically. My friend just smiled, maybe to indicate his approval, boredom or his incomprehensibility.

In simple words, revenge is our act of reacting to pain, insult or loss caused to us by others. A boy rejected in love, a woman deceived by her man, a businessman cheated by his partner, an adolescent insulted by his classmates, a poor victim of bribe and corruption in the society, a nation defeated by another nation - all think of taking revenge in their own way.

Revenge is usually a by-product of pain followed by anger. It may be a trick of the mind to divert you and bring you out from the present sadness. Initially, you arrive at a temporary decision of taking revenge. It's all good as long as the decision you take in anger lives for a short time. The decision normally dies before you convert it into action. But sometimes, the decisions escape death and live on.

In pain and anger, we lose the track of right thought process. We generalize incorrectly. We lose trust in ALL the girls, ALL the men, the entire education system, the whole marriage institution, complete humanity, or society on the whole. Then starts the process of teaching the RIGHT lesson to the people, to the society, to the system and to the whole world.

The boy rejected by a girl seeks shelter of alcohol in the bar. In extreme cases, he may plan an acid attack on the girl. The woman deceived by her man attempts suicide or may file a case legally. The business person may plan to murder his partner. The man betrayed by his wife may plan to kill her and her partner or he may knock on some other door. The student insulted by his classmates and teachers may develop hatred towards the subject or the whole education system and starts repelling from the school. An office colleague who wants to take revenge may just spread some vague rumours and try to defame you. The victim of corruption in society may take a gun and become a Naxalite. The relatives may opt for black magic or witchcraft causing harm in the name of revenge.

What's wrong with taking revenge for the insults we face, pains we suffer from and deceptions that we encounter? Well, it's not wrong to take revenge, but most of the time, we don't ensure that our purpose of revenge is served properly.

The rejected boy spoils his health and life by becoming an alcoholic. The student ruins his own career just because some classmates or a teacher insulted him. How is committing suicide serving any purpose for a wife who is cheated on by her husband? She just loses her life. The man who kills or plans to kill his wife along with her partner just spends his years behind the bars.

Spoiling our career and life in the name of revenge is not wisdom. Have you ever seen a doctor taking medicine for a patient's disease? We fail to understand this. We treat ourselves and make ourselves victims in the game of revenge.

Even in extreme cases of anger and sadness, I have devised a process of a revenge plan.

First: will I be badly affected if I take this revenge?

Second: In the name of taking revenge, am I planning to affect only the person/group or even their dependents or loved ones?

Third: Can I take my revenge furthermore and target the cause instead of targeting the person?

Fourth: How much I am responsible for this pain or insult by others that are making me plan to take revenge?

Fifth and foremost: Is it really necessary to take revenge? Does that person even deserve my revenge or should I just ignore it and move on?

I know it's hard to think of all these points when we are extremely sad or angry. Well, that's what differentiates you from other ordinary people. It's wise to ask these questions at least after our mood calms down a bit. Believe me! Most of the time, we will drop the idea of taking revenge after this thought process.

Does it mean that we should not take revenge even when the other person hurts, insults or does a mistake? Certainly not! But our revenge should be creative in approach, enriching our lives and possibly creating healthy guilt and teaching a lesson to the person you want to take revenge on.

Raising your voice is the weakest act. Silence needs great strength. Be strong and remain silent. People who insult expect you to shout, argue, retaliate, fight back and bring you down to their level. Give them a shock. Remain silent and ignore. There is no better pain than being neglected.

Love and loyalty are great qualities that cannot be expected in return from everyone. Well, it is hard to accept when we are deceived. Dying is not the answer. Killing is not a solution. When someone doesn't value your bonding and can go ahead seeking someone else, it is foolish to think that you can take revenge by hurting them back by Knocking on the other door. It doesn't hurt them when there is no such emotional bonding. Indeed, in the process of taking revenge, you will hurt yourself by going out of your character and acting like someone else. Divert yourself. Ignore. Remain yourself. If one day, the person who deceived you may feel guilty for cheating on you. There is no bigger punishment than this. Move on. Time heals everything.

We encounter insults related to our appearance, our caste, colour, financial status, educational background and so on. Let's check what's in our hands and what's beyond. Think about what needs to be fixed and what should be ignored.

If someone insults my physical appearance, I can either spoil his physical appearance by splashing acid on his face or I can demonstrate that I can earn more respect through my words, actions, attitude and behaviour than I could earn through appearance. When I know spoiling his appearance doesn't beautify me, I choose the second option. I can target the person or I can address the cause. Success is the best revenge.

The right way to handle the stone that you stumbled upon while walking on a road is by throwing it aside, learning to be careful from then and continuing walking, not hitting it back and getting hurt again.

One day when you look back, you will realize your silence, negligence and success were far more sensible, creative, effective and right means of revenge. Poor people! They have given you pain and insults. Repay the debt. Give them the gift of repentance for losing someone so good like you.

Whenever I would pretend angry or upset and scold my little girl for her deeds, after a very short time, she would come from behind and hug me. What a lovely revenge!

CHAPTER TWENTY-ONE

WHOM DO YOU WANT TO BE?

Only one lotus braved the blast of winter and bloomed in the garden of Sudas the gardener. He took it to sell to the King. A traveller said to him on the way, "I will buy this untimely flower, and take it to my master Buddha. Ask your price." The gardener asked one golden masha, and the traveller readily agreed. Just then the King came there. "I must take that lotus to Lord Buddha," he said to the gardener. "What is your price?"

The gardener claimed two golden mashas. The King was ready to buy it. The traveller doubled the price and the King's offer ran still higher. The gardener thought in his greed he could get much more from the man for whom they were eagerly bidding.

He hastened with his flower to the grove where Buddha sat silent. Love shone in his eyes, on his lips was wisdom beyond words. Sudas gazed at him, and stood still. Suddenly he fell on his knees, placing the lotus at Buddha's feet. Buddha smiled and asked, "What is your prayer, my son?" "Nothing, my lord," Sudas answered "only a speck of the dust off your feet.'

*****

That's how Gurudev Tagore ends the story and my wandering in the story begins. For me, it's not the story of devotion, not the story of greed, nor the story of wisdom; it's about finding out who I am in the story and who I should be. We remain just the readers of some stories, but we want to become the characters in others. The real confusion and contemplation start there.

Should we become the gardener? One who is the owner of the lotus? He did what other gardeners might also have done. Owning a garden and watering plants every day. He did not do any extra effort. But he understood how precious the flower is, he knew how to handle it in the best way, and he knew where he would get the best value for it. In the end, he realized what's the actual best value he can get. Should we become the gardener?

Should we become the Lotus which is the root point of the entire story? It stood different from other flowers. It dared to bloom against all the odds of the season when all the other buds were sleeping, unwilling to blossom being in their comfort zone. It showed that one who dares to risk, dares to question and overcomes the odds gets great value. Should we become the Lotus?

Should we become the traveller? He was the one who was ready to pay a price higher than the King to devote the Lotus to his Master Buddha. He had a sense of devotion and gratefulness towards Buddha and wanted to express it by offering a rare flower without caring about the higher price he had decided to pay. He was the one who dared to compete even with a King to show his devotion towards his master. Should we become the traveller?

Should we become the King? He is the one, who, being the head of the kingdom, did not exercise his power to snatch the flower, but instead, bid for the flower fairly with the gardener. He too, like the gardener was devoted towards and grateful to Lord Buddha and wanted to express that by offering this rare flower. Should we become the King?

Should we become the golden masha? That is the money that tried to buy the effort of the flower in blooming against all odds. That is the money that tried to buy the smartness of the gardener. That is the money that made the traveller and the king think that devotion can be expressed with something that can be bought by it. Should we become the golden masha?

Finally, should we become Buddha? One who had seen and undergone the pain and effort of the lotus, one who had seen the greed of many such gardeners, one who had experienced the devotion of thousands of such travellers and kings, one who had dropped millions of such golden mashas and one who had come to the grove, away from everyone, beyond everyone and one who answered all of these with just a smile and shine in his eyes. Should we become Buddha?

Maybe you should remain you. Maybe you should remain a question without even seeking an answer.

THE BIRD AND THE CAGE

A birdcatcher cast his net, caught a bird, brought it home and caged it in a newly brought cage.

"Are you cruel by birth?" asked the bird to the cage.

I don't know. This is the first time I have ever bound someone in me," answered the cage innocently and honestly.

Within a day's time, the bird felt suffocated in the cage for not having the freedom to fly wherever it wanted.

I hate you for what you are doing," said the bird curtly.

"I'm just doing my job, but I'm liking your company," added the cage, "Well, if you are so much frustrated with my company, I'll tell you a trick: you can just lift the door from the bottom and I'll be opened."

"Isn't it against your responsibility to let me free?" asked the bird.

"Well, yes it is, but it's against my heart to hold you tightly when you want to fly away. The guilt of being irresponsible is less painful compared to the pain of snatching your freedom," said the cage.

The bird flew away.

****

A couple of days passed. The bird flew over the hills, surfed over the waves of rivers, fluttered its wings in joy, eating the fruits and worms it liked, roamed in the skies it always loved. "Freedom is life's ultimate joy," thought the bird.

The birdcatcher caught it again, brought it back home and caged it.

Although the bird was upset, it was not as sad as it was earlier.

"In a way, I'm happy that you are back, but I know you are not," said the cage.

"Maybe!" replied the bird.

"But this time the birdcatcher has put a small latch at my door. I'm afraid I can't help you to escape unless I fall down from the height and the latch opens itself," the cage expressed its helplessness.

The days passed. The bird and the cage started exchanging the stories of their birth, their lives before they reached here and so on. They inevitably became each other's company. But the bird had some incomplete feeling.

"I have no happiness. I miss my people, my fellow birds," said the bird one day.

"Do they love you so much? Do you love them so much?" asked the cage.

"I don't know, but I am used to their company. I belong there," answered the bird.

"Just flutter your wings and I'll fall down. Let's see if the latch opens. If it does, you can then fly away to your people," said the cage.

"Doesn't falling down hurt you?" the bird asked.

"It hurts, but not as much as keeping you caged here, having your physical presence here and seeing you miss your people."

The bird fluttered its wings and the cage fell down. The latch opened. The bird flew away.

******

The bird found happiness in finding its flock and joining its fellow birds in flying to far distances in search of food. While the birds were happy to see this bird back at first, gradually it became just one among all. It was not life; it was just existence. It was not living; it was just survival.

The bird just remembered the cage and felt that it should go back and meet the cage once. It parted from the flock and flew back.

*****

"Come! I was expecting you!" said the cage without much surprise as if it knew the bird's return.

"Did you know I would return? What made you think that I would return?" questioned the bird.

"Well, you went in search of happiness. Happiness doesn't exist without love. Love doesn't blossom in indifference. In the flock, I could guess, you would be just 'someone to everyone and everyone is just someone to you'."

The bird didn't seem to understand it fully. It just smiled and entered the cage.

*****

The birdcatcher took the bird along with the cage to the weekly fair. A man who was against caging animals and birds bought the bird along with the cage, took it home and opened the cage. The bird didn't fly.

"Why don't you want to fly? Don't you want freedom and happiness?" - asked the man.

"I don't want to be someone to everyone. I can't be with everyone who is just someone to me. I find happiness in being with one who is one only to me and I want to be with one to whom I'm the only one." answered the bird.

The cage didn't get closed and the bird never flew away thereafter.

CHAPTER TWENTY-THREE

PROMOTIONS AND EMOTIONS

'There are politics wherever you go!' – is the ultimate workplace enlightenment in almost everyone's professional life.

By the time we realize the pasture on the other side of the hill is just as green as (or as dry as) the one here, we would have spent more than half of our life. We realize that there is the same competition, there are same types of people and there are the same politics wherever we go!

Sometimes we strongly believe (or sense) that someone or some people around us are conspiring against our professional growth. We feel that our hard work is not being recognized. Our commitment towards work, our proficiency, subject matter expertise, system knowledge and experience are going in vain.

Actually, what stops or hampers our professional growth? How do we think and react to the circumstances we face? What stops us from flying?

The answer is: WING, WIND and SKY

Most of us develop World Is Not Good (WING) attitude over a period of time when we don't get what we expect. Our very kind ego doesn't want us to feel inferior in our own sight. It invokes the fox within us that comes to the conclusion: unreachable grapes are sour.

We start blaming every other possible individual as the reason for not being able to grow. We start speaking the jargon built for such situations: I can clearly see 'favouritism' by the boss. That executive is an expert in 'bucketing'. That team leader knows how to apply 'butter' to get her work done by the manager. I am always 'being targeted'.

And the master of all: 'There are politics here!'

While some or all of these points are partially true in some workplaces, our WING attitude blocks us from looking at anything good and thinking of steps or alternatives to grow. Everything appears yellowish to our jaundiced eyes. We neither learn to be blind towards negativity around us nor do we just walk out of such an unpleasant atmosphere. We keep blaming, complaining and still keep dwelling in the same place.

Next is the WIND (Why I'm not deserving?) attitude. It's exactly the opposite of the WING. We unnecessarily start developing a feeling of inferiority about ourselves and start questioning 'Am I incapable?' Well! It's good to stand outside ourselves and introspect, however, in this phase of disappointment we generally do not ask the question 'Am I incapable?' to find out about true strengths and weaknesses. But we just ask this as a way of hurting ourselves more.

Again, while some of the time it is true that we may be lacking some of the qualities or qualifications, it is not always our 'lacking' that stops our growth. With such a disturbed mindset, we simply lose our existing confidence. Gradually the question 'Am I incapable?' turns into the statement 'I am incapable.' We start believing what is not true; or, we stop trying to overcome our shortcomings. The best conclusion is not to come to any conclusion, especially when you feel bad about yourself.

Even if the World is good and even if You are good, sometimes we don't get what we expect: The SKY (Skills, Knowledge and the Y-factor)

Every profession needs some job-related skills and knowledge. And then we have a term called X-factor. X-factor is some unexplainable spark that is hidden in an individual that makes him or her get noticed and helps grow. Out of many models, one model attracts the jury; out of many background dancers, one girl somehow gets noticed by the choreographer, out of many students one boy grabs the attention of the teacher – it's difficult to define why! We call it X-factor.

Can we practise or cultivate the X-factor? Maybe yes! By being active, by doing something more meaningfully, gracefully and differently, we may earn that X-factor. But we come across something called Y-factor. And this plays stupid tricks. It has nothing to do with your skill, your knowledge, your X-factor, your experience, dedication. It spoils the entire game.

A company makes a policy not to appoint or promote unmarried girls even if they have all the qualifications needed for the post. A manager does not recommend his subordinate's name for the post of Assistant Manager with the foresight that the subordinate would overtake him. A team leader decides not to promote newlywed women with the fear that they may take longer maternity leave. A lady with excellent subject knowledge and teaching skills gets rejected for the post of the teacher merely because of her appearance. Another manager keeps a very eligible employee aside and brings HIS people to that place. How do we address such Y-factors? Well, that's a million-dollar question.

One, fold the WING attitude and let it not flutter. It's hard to practise but we should be wise enough to choose the right lens. Most of the time, the size of the good and bad things around us are not as big or small as they actually are. We look at problems with magnifiers and we wear an opaque glass while looking at happiness. Being blind to negatives may not dissolve the problems, but will make you use your energy towards finding a solution.

Two, stop the WIND attitude. There is no point in blaming, doubting and thereby punishing yourself. Many times you are a basketball trying to fit yourself into the golf field hole. You are in the wrong place! Isn't it foolishness for a basketball to compare itself with a golf one? If we truly are unfit for something and you have identified it, the war is half won. We have identified the drawback and it's all about working on it.

Y-factor? How can you expect growth from someone so mean, selfish and senseless? The world is not small. The world is not all bad. If they have someone else to wrongly fit in your place, you also have someone else who places you where you fit rightly.

If a flower has a hundred bees; a bee has a thousand flowers.

Every day, without your knowledge, through good and bad experiences, life is exposing you to new learning and new experience. And that will surely count and help sometime, somewhere in future.

If none of the above solutions makes sense, look around; there are people with the same problem. Comfort yourself by saying that you are not alone.

CHAPTER TWENTY-FOUR

SEEING THAT INVISIBLE LINE

We sound boring and irritating and we encounter failures not because we do not start doing, but because we fail to understand where and when to stop. Most of the times we fail to see the invisible line. We just cross it, then repent and make a lot of circus to get back. Sometimes we succeed but most of the times we fail.

Our body, our common sense, our conscience and the people around us give a lot of indications of the line. We just ignore the warnings and cross that line. It's once again our body, our ego and some other people who encourage us to ignore and cross the line. We create a dirty defence mechanism within us and ignore the warnings.

The stomach knows what quantity of food is needed to manage the body. But the tongue dominates and sends the decision of eating some more when food is tasty. We suffer indigestion.

Wisdom knows what should be spoken and how much should be spoken on the stage. But our illusion of 'I know everything' or our identity crisis of 'No one identifies me' makes us speak even after the content is over. We start sounding boring.

Our intellect knows that love for each other is dead in our relationship, but our heart keeps hoping that the love would return. The dead body of our relationship starts stinking.

A male colleague makes a joke that creates discomfort among the lady colleagues in the group, a girl suffering from an identity crisis speaks more than needed during some friends' gathering, a woman unnecessarily tries to bargain the time to look younger than she is and takes the shelter of heavy make-up and irrelevant costumes to her age. They all forget that there is a line not to be crossed.

We can sound sensible even by speaking less but meaningfully. We become wiser when we know whom and what to hold on to and when to say Goodbye to instead of trying forever unnecessarily. We can look beautiful by being simple and keeping ourselves age-appropriate.

We just mismanage our body, personality and emotions in us without knowing where the invisible line is. Maturity is all about seeing that invisible line.

CHAPTER TWENTY-FIVE

Every Great Leader Erases That Line

It sounds stupid when someone says something like "Don't mix up your professional and personal life", or "Don't take it personally; the comment is about your profession, not about you" or "Don't let your personal matters affect your profession."

We accept such statements just because they are popular and they are often told by people whom we consider highly knowledgeable.

You are a person on the whole – a collection of your knowledge, your emotions, your logic, your experiences, your thought process, your beliefs, your ideas and so on. All your thoughts and actions (or reactions) are based on them – whether at home, at the workplace, or any other public place.

We have one brain. Although it is divided into two halves (surely, not one half for personal and another for professional use), what we perceive through our senses, what we store as memory, what we infer out of available information, how we receive some experiences – everything happens irrespective of place. And we use all that for our responses or reactions in future.

I may sound too simple, but here's an example for easy understanding. We touch a hot surface at home. It burns our hand and our brain's reflex mechanism immediately withdraws the hand from that surface. Does it happen differently at our workplace if we touch a hot surface?

We may think, that's about physical experience and reaction. But, it happens in the same way even in emotional and intellectual aspects; maybe the degree and ways differ, but the root perception and reactions remain the same.

You may react 'on spot' in one way when your mother scolds you at home and you may react in some other way when your higher-up insults you at your workplace. That's because the liberty to retaliate and shout back at home is more compared to doing the same at the workplace. But the root emotions, either anger or sadness, are generated in both places. We just choose to express them in different ways and at different degrees.

Now, all this said, what's the use of knowing that there is no bifurcation between the personal way and the professional way?

Well, it helps you to be the better version of yourself – everywhere. We must first understand that 'emotions' are not meant for personal life alone and 'orderliness' is not meant just for the workplace. It's important to add 'emotions' at work and 'orderliness' in personal life; just knowing the right amount to use and the right place to stop applying them.

No great leader is ever made without investing emotions in his or her team. The leader may be highly knowledgeable, superbly skilled, truly talented, but if there is no emotional connect, the team spirit never rises. No matter what way the team members are motivated through incentives and positions, it does not last long. It all works on the basic understanding that the leader is handling people, not machines. So, it doesn't take fuel or power, it takes emotions.

Applying emotions does not reduce your work, but it surely eases the pressure and keeps the boredom, monotony, mechanicalistic viewpoint towards work.

Just answer yourself. Imagine that a newly joined team member, who looks exactly like your brother and treats you the same way, comes a little late to work. Can you be as harsh as you are with other team members? Assume that your manager, who speaks exactly like your uncle who brought you up with great care from your childhood days, questions or scolds you in a team meeting. Do you develop that anger, grudge or get sad about it for a long time?

Well, all that happens when we look at those people only professionally connected. A small shift in the way you look at your team members – either higher-ups, peers or subordinates – can create wonders in people management. All the great leaders I have seen have this emotional bonding and all the bad leaders I have seen clcarly drcw a linc between emotions and work!

A strict boss could be compared to an angry uncle in your family. A childlike girl in your team could be your niece at home. A middle-aged housekeeping employee at the workplace could be your aunt in faraway relatives.

The moment they appear like that and from the time our viewpoints act like that, we tend to look at their positives, we ignore their minor mistakes, we forgive them quickly when they speak something harshly out of their pressure, we don't get offended and don't carry the same mood for a long time even if they are not all right with us, we teach them, we learn from them, we care for them. Their small appreciation matters and our small concern touches them. That's how you create a happy aura around you at your workplace – as a leader and as a team member.

There is no line between personal and professional ways. But we must understand, there is always a line to be drawn on what extent and how emotions and orderliness can be mixed in personal and professional areas.

We need to understand that there are ethics and sensitivity on both sides. Just because someone looks like a brother at the workplace, we ought not do him a special favour at work. Just because a team member looks like your niece, we cannot cross the limits of decency. Just because we should treat people as our own, we must not think we own them and start interfering in every personal matter and become 'Uchita Salahananda Swami'!

The popularity earned by keeping our ethics aside can never become respect. A fatherly leader who teaches skills needed to grow is respected more compared to an unethical boss who promotes someone just because that someone belongs to the same caste or looks like someone in the family.

Nothing great has ever been achieved on this planet without love and without spreading happiness. I'm sure our home and our workplace - both are on this planet.

CHAPTER TWENTY-SIX

THE CORRECTION FACTOR

My uncle was lying almost unconscious on the deathbed. The doctor checked the blood pressure and I could see the reading on the digital sphygmomanometer clearly as 140/90. The doctor said 'It's 110/75 which is more or less normal.'

Maybe the doctor could read the question on my face and started explaining 'Since it is a digital device, we should reduce the systolic (numerator) value by 30 and diastolic (denominator) by 15. So, 140/90 should be understood as 110/75.' Although I was not so much keen or concerned about the reason or explanation at that time, perhaps that was stored somewhere in my brain to pop up later.

Don't we have to understand such 'correction factors' related to people and circumstances in our day-to-day as well?

You may have come across some people who exaggerate everything. To describe their ancestors who hardly had a 3BHK house and a few acres of land, they say 'My grandfather used to keep a gold foil, the real gold foil on hot boiled rice in his plate and would let it melt and mix in the rice and eat it at every meal. But my father spent all the money on gambling, horse race and parties in just 5 years.' Some people even glorify their poverty: 'When we were children, we hardly used to get a meal once a week. Then I decided to grow rich. Today you name anything, I have it at my house.' Some people find pleasure in overrating diseases also: 'My friend was smoking 80 – 100 cigarettes every day. He didn't listen to us and he died a dog's death by vomiting 1 – 2 litres of blood every day during the last few days of his life.'

We call it Hyperbole – a figure of speech in the English language.

We have another category of people who are opposite. They are so inert, so disinterested and so unexcited about life.

Even when their friend meets with a serious accident with a damaged head, fractured bones and bruised bleeding body, they just say 'Well, the bike just skidded and there are some minor scratches and small injuries. Nothing to worry about.' A marriage broker says, about his client 'the boy is a little social, has some friends and negligible hobbies which are common these days and is pampered child of his parents; everything will be streamlined once he gets into married life' to actually describe a boy who is a serious drug addict, who is a parasite snatching money from his parents and has friends with a criminal background. Even an ordinary writer (one who records complaints) at a police station speaks like an expert and experienced police officer about some horrific and serial killings in the town as 'These are common. I have seen many such cases in my experience.'

We call it 'Understatement' - again, a figure of speech in the English language.

Why do people exaggerate or understate anything?

Well, although exaggeration and understatement seem the opposite, the reasons behind them are common. Category one: usually such people have an identity crisis and need to seek attention. Two: such people just want to get some benefit out of it by speaking like that.

After you judge that they are either exaggerating or understating, category one people become too irritating. All we can do is just ignore them and keep our distance from them.

There is another problem if we don't judge them and their words. We tend to make wrong decision and take incorrect actions. We may just ignore a disease that needs an immediate attention and treatment if a person understates its symptoms. We may get panic even for a negligible problem if we hear it from someone who exaggerates.

If we don't judge properly, the real problem will be with people who exaggerate or understate for their benefit for their selfish motives. We may fall prey to their words. Attend any chain marketing meetings, they start with exaggerated words like 'Do you want to be the owner of such Audi Q7 car in next 2 years?' or understated words like: 'Tata Punch? Mercedes GLA? Forget them. Even the Audi Q7 car can be easily bought by the way you make money with our simple marketing plan!"

It's stupidity to stick to the 'Don't be judgemental' rule! We have to judge people. Your judgement may go false and you may arrive at a different judgement later, but we must judge. Judgement is simply a process of observing something or someone keenly and arriving at a conclusion whether they suit us or not!

It's not in our control to stop people from exaggerating or understating anything. They always either add more to the original or remove some essence from the original. But we have 'the correction factor' in our control.

Through proper observation and judgement, we must practice applying the correction factor. It is simply the difference between 'What they say' and 'what it actually means'. As we do this, we will understand, what they describe something as 'a crime' is actually just a common mistake, what they call something as 'just a compromise' is actually 'lifetime suffering'.

It's very dangerous if we don't apply the correction factor when people speak about us. When anyone says 'You are extraordinary', I know I should apply the correction factor and reduce it to 'You are just above ordinary' and when someone says 'You are fit for nothing' I should apply the correction factor again and say to myself 'I know, I don't fit everything, but I'm sure something fits me and I fit many things.'

Amid all these, there are some people who neither try to seek your attention nor they have any selfish motive. Their words simply come out of love and creativity. Accept their exaggeration and take their understatement without any correction factors.

CHAPTER TWENTY-SEVEN

BACKFIRE CALLED OVERTHINKING

I remember a joke read long back:

A sardar asked his son:

"How was your English test?"

"It was easy except for one bit: the Past Participle form of the word think is ___________," said the son.

"What did you write?"

"I thought, thought, thought for a long time and then wrote thunk," answered the genius son.

*****

Don't think too much if you didn't understand the joke; it was just about a strange disorder called overthinking.

Let's look at a set of statements:

Time is very sensitive. What if I catch a cold, let me close the window. Life is very uncertain. What if I lose my job tomorrow, let me start saving money as much as I can. The world is very bad. What if my children get into bad company and learn bad practices, let me not let them go out so much. People are too exploitative. What if they start borrowing money if I get closer to them, let me maintain some distance. My body is too vulnerable to diseases and infections, let me not eat or drink water outside.

The lines above are about a strange mental state called worrying.

We come across many people (sometimes including ourselves) who overthink or worry. Overthinking in its correct form is just 'thinking' which is the root of human evolution. But overthinking is a backfire. The same is the case with over-worrying. When it is in the right amount, it is called 'precariousness' or just 'being careful before something adverse happens', but when it goes to extremes, it becomes 'worrying'.

Overthinking is mostly related to intelligence and over-worrying can be intellectual or emotional. Whatsoever, both are the unwanted children of our thought process.

What's wrong if we overthink?

Let me drive this with an analogy of filling a bucket with water. Assume that an empty bucket is a problem or a life situation. Filling water is 'thinking'. The bucket has a finite capacity and so are the problems that need finite attention and thinking. What happens if we keep filling the water even after the bucket is full? Water spills out. That's exactly how overthinking works. There's no use; indeed it's wasteful or a loss. Every problem, every issue, every concern, every unexpected situation in life needs just a finite level of thinking. Anything that we overdo starts acting against us.

Another problem with overthinking is not acting towards the solution. Thinking should stop at the right time and action (towards a solution) should start from that point. But if we keep thinking even after crossing the required level, we are wasting time and not moving towards a solution.

It may sound strange but overthinking becomes a part of our personality if we do not identify and stop it. The most challenging part is to identify the stop spot. It is difficult to find where to stop thinking. If it is considered a bigger problem or a decision to take, it is always good to draw a flow chart of your thoughts on a paper in the form of Possibilities/Plans and their pros and cons. If I follow Plan A, what are the challenges and what are the conveniences? Similarly for plan B. Then check doable actions and assign priorities. If we have to gain or lose something out of available options, what it should be? By writing it on a paper (or any other media), we see an endpoint for thinking. Then start acting on your plan.

Sometimes even small matters provoke us to overthink. They become worries. A mother starts thinking hard if her daughter doesn't return home on time. Did she miss the bus or did her bike break down? Did she get any unexpected work? She could have made a call. Has her phone's battery got drained? Maybe network issues? – All this flow of thoughts sounds okay. If her arrival still gets delayed, thoughts get converted into worries. Accident? Any undesired act while passing through remote places? Worries start sounding like strong possibilities. It's always good not to wait until our overthinking gets converted into worries. Once we cross that borderline, our thought process goes out of the logic track. The only way to get out of that phase is a two-line mantra: *Stop worrying. Start acting.* Although it may sound like a consoling saying, but in such situations, it's always good to tell ourselves 'No news is good news'.

The stupidest part is assumptive worry. Well, in fact, all the worries are just assumptions without factual information. But some worries are totally needless. Packing some paracetamol tablets while going on a trip is fine. That's a precaution. But do we take a physician along with us? That becomes worrying. Not everything can be planned in life. Sometimes we have to act spontaneously. Look at a funny story:

A newly married man invited his colleagues for lunch assuming that his wife cooks well. When he informed previous night, she told that she knows nothing except cooking lemon rice.

They made a plan. He told his wife "Well, you prepare only lemon rice. But when they come for lunch, just keep dropping empty vessels one after the other in the kitchen. From the dining hall, I keep asking what fell down. Every time keep telling a dish slipped out of your hand. At last I will ask what is left. You just tell lemon rice. I will pretend to be angry and ask you to serve the same.'

The plan sounded great.

Next day, when his colleagues arrived, the couple was about to start the drama. As planned, he heard the sound of a dropping vessel.

He asked 'What's that?'

To his shock, his wife said in confusion 'Please come here.'

When he went inside, he saw that the very vessel with lemon rice had indeed fallen down.

*****

Not everything goes as we plan even with utmost precaution. It's foolish to worry that drinking tap water would cause infection even when food is choked in the throat when bottled water is not available nearby. It's stupid to lose the joy of getting drenched in rain and worrying that we may catch a cold. Life's tasteless if we worry too much and keep ourselves away from street food once in a while with the fear of adding cholesterol to our veins. It's insane to worry that the prices would hike and we may not be able to build a house after some years and then start building a house, taking a heavy home loan and paying EMIs for the next hundred years of your life.

It's okay to think and even worry about the true problems or suffering that exists. But it's sheer foolishness to overthink and worry about something that is far unlikely to happen. It's stupidity to drive away the existing happiness and invite suffering. Wisdom is all about seeing those lines between carelessness and over-precariousness, between thinking and overthinking. Some lines appear to our inner eyes. Some lines can be seen through spectacles of others' experiences. Sometimes we cross the line and get the sight. Today's problems will become tomorrow's jokes. Today's worries will be tomorrow's pastime fun. Life gets life when we realize it's not worth taking so seriously.

CHAPTER TWENTY-EIGHT

THE PAIN SPEAKING...

On the tables of liquor bars, in the moaning of labour rooms, in the stories of old age homes, in the words of suicide notes, inside the cells of jails, in the silence of the house of death, in the lines of tragic love songs – only one emotion rules: the pain.

Pain is sometimes physical and sometimes emotional. Unlike shameless and purposeless happiness, most of the pains come with their own dignity and purpose.

When it is physical, pain is a mechanism of telling our brain that some part of the body is damaged and needs attention. It may be a cut, a bruise, a burn or a complete breaking of something. The brain immediately makes arrangements like blocking blood loss.

But emotional pain is more complex. The body has very limited faculties to handle it or maybe our stupidity acquired externally from our civilization, our societies and our education prevent our body from handling emotional pains well.

We fail to handle pains for many reasons.

One, we do not understand and accept the reason for pain. When we encounter pain, we fail to sit back for some time and find the root cause. A boy rejected by a girl, a woman cheated on by her husband, a student failed in an exam and so on forget that they, directly or indirectly are the reason for their own pains. Some of such pains give the option of coming out of them with some alternatives. We just need to think without being emotional. When emotions have locked you in a room of pain, you cannot ask the same emotions to open the lock. Make the key available to your intelligence.

Two, we knock on the wrong doors for coming out of the pain. Like we have painkillers for physical pains, we have painkillers for emotional pains too. We pour the liquor into the tumblers of our weaker minds. We seek solutions for our pains on the tables of bars. We ring the bells of temples to drive away the pain. We seek God's help who is neither the reason, nor the witness, nor the victim to understand our pain and drive it away. The pain hides until the liquor is present in our body and returns as soon as we are sober. God can never replace your loved one. At the last level, we knock on the doors of death; we commit suicide. We decide to come out of life permanently instead of coming out of temporary pain. It's not the lack of windows to happiness, it is the unwillingness to open the windows that keeps us in pain.

Three, strangely we start retaining the pain and enjoy self-pity without understanding that every pain has a validity period and a purpose. We sometimes start enjoying people's sympathy for our pain. We start getting disconnected from the world intentionally with the fear of losing pain. We make all possible efforts to keep the pain with us by retaining all the memories of people who left us or whom we lost. We listen to the songs that keep the pain alive. We glorify our pain and decide to live with it without realizing that life is meant to live. We forget that we should send off pain after its validity is over. We become deaf to life's calls. We become blind to the best healer: time.

Four, in contrary to the case above, we try to escape or get rid of the pain as soon as possible. We try to stretch our hands too early towards some solutions and some people, to get rid of the pain given by others, mostly to take revenge. But, that is not how pain operates. Pain is like fog in the air in the morning. It takes its own time to get cleared. The best way to come out of pain is to accept and be in the pain until it completes its work. We must know that some damages are beyond repair and some people are beyond replacement. When we lose them or when they leave us, life feels shattered. That's when the pain comes to play its role. The pain has to clearly register in your mind that the person's role or that time is over and does not come back. And this registering takes time. If you do not let the pain do its work or hurry up in getting out of pain and seek some alternatives, the loss does not get registered properly and you may try seeking and searching for them again just to get disappointed again. Instead, let the pain register the loss fully in us. It's okay to cry out loud and let pain rule you until its purpose is served.

Any pain is more painful only when we either try to retain it for longer than it should or when we try to get rid of it sooner than it completes its job. Give pain the time and value it deserves, neither more nor less.

The real value of pain is seen after it leaves us. It becomes a memory. It becomes a lesson. It becomes an experience. It becomes a torch for the paths we walk.

CHAPTER TWENTY-NINE

EGO: MIND'S SKELETAL SYSTEM

The same question was given to both of them.

Fill in the blank space:

______ should I fix the spoiling relationship?

The first candidate 'maturity' fin illed the blank with the word 'How'. That meant: How should I fix the spoiling relationship?

The other candidate filled in the blank with 'Why'. Why should I fix the spoiling relationship?

The name of the second candidate is 'Ego'.

While maturity knows 'what' is important, the 'ego' just asks 'who' is important. And the answer is always 'I'.

*****

Just imagine some day-to-day situations:

The security guard of your office building doesn't greet you when you pass by even after seeing you. A relative much younger than you doesn't even offer a seat to you when he sees you at a party. A random auto-driver makes a loose comment on your value during an unnecessary argument. The husband who lived together for thirty years takes the side of the newly arrived daughter-in-law, instead of supporting his wife during a debate at home. Although you are important, your name is forgotten in a ceremony at the office or on an invitation card of a relative's wedding. A colleague with much lesser experience gets more increment or early promotion compared to you.

How do you feel? Sad? Angry? Or Do you just ignore and remain indifferent?

Most of us get angry or sad in such situations, because of the 'ego' that's sitting somewhere inside rules our thought process and reaction at that moment.

Our Ego is hurt.

Let's imagine some other situations:

'Not sure why, but you are looking gorgeous today,' a colleague or classmate gives an unexpected compliment. 'Truly you spoke so powerfully today, sir. From now, the opposition leaders will think before they comment,' says a politician's follower. 'Look at her handwriting; it's so neat,' praises a teacher of a little girl in the classroom. 'Who can understand me so well other than you? I don't know what would happen to me if you weren't there,' says a husband in the emotional flow.

The above praising words are not necessarily false. They may be honest. The matter is: such words of appreciation boost one's ego. The ego of the beauty, the politician, the little girl, and the wife is boosted.

The majority of us think that the word 'ego' is bad by itself. And we use that in the same context. But that's not true. In fact, ego is absolutely needed in everyone.

Observe carefully: whenever we felt miserably lonely, when we feel irrecoverably lost, horribly useless to the world when we feel the world is pushing us away and death is calling us close, when we feel we have failed in studies, job or relationships, it is the same ego that stretches its hands and helps us stand up.

When you fail in a college exam, the ego that consoles you reminding you of your success in school, when you are rejected in a job interview, the ego that fills confidence reminding you of your skills to get other jobs, when a relationship is broken, the ego that cheers you up justifying that you did everything possible to hold it, when you feel inferior comparing yourself with your friends in higher positions, the ego that makes you feel proud of the ways you are carrying out responsibilities at home.. all this ego is truly essential. You call it consolation, false justification, overconfidence, or self-esteem, but all these are different faces of a healthy ego. In such situations, your mind needs ego like your body needs a skeletal system to stand upright without collapsing.

If one doesn't have such a healthy ego, he falls into depression. In extremes, he may even say goodbye to life.

Our intelligent mental system makes every possible attempt to keep such ego active in us. The woman who fills her eyes and appreciates her beauty every time when she stands in front of the mirror, the girl who uploads her photos and videos on social screens and gets boosted with likes and hearts, the boy who is obsessed with his bike, gym and looks, everyone through their song, their speech, their art, their achievements – keep doing the same work, unknowingly: keeping a healthy ego active in them.

But the problem starts when we cross the limit of a healthy ego. The ego is like a food preservative in packaged food. It should exist only to the level of keeping the food from spoiling. If it exceeds, the same food preservative becomes the poison that spoils the food. Such excess ego changes the language of a person.

'Are you so great that you started advising me?' questions the father to his son. 'I know how to handle it; I don't need to learn this from you,' speaks a lady harshly to her colleague. 'I have seen so many people like you. I don't care,' we make such statements in the heat of the moment with our neighbours.

Sometimes we go a step ahead and degrade others by their appearance, financial status, job, familial conditions, caste and religion.

All these are the symptoms of excess ego accumulated in us. The ego is meant to stay within us and support us like a bone. But we bring it out and use it like a stick to beat and hurt others for undue reasons.

Such ego halts our wisdom, stops us from being sensitive to others' emotions, kills humanity, develops anger and drives away happiness. With such ego, we start feeling superior to others. We start dominating. We expect others to accept and follow us because we think we are right. If two people have such an ego, it kills the relationship between them. Even if one of them has such an ego, the other cannot keep boosting the ego of the other and one day, the relationship eventually dies.

Two ego-cutters that act as the solution are one, love and the other logical thinking. Love addresses our emotional ego while logical thinking regulates our intellectual ego.

Why shouldn't someone younger than us advise us? They may know more than us. Is anyone at our workplace not respecting us? It may not be their excess ego. Are you acting in a way that earns respect from others? We usually don't question ourselves.

Love is the only spectacle that makes the vision clear when ego blurs our mind. Unless our mind's feet don't fit others' mind's footwear, we cannot have a pleasant walk together. Only love makes your mind's feet elastic.

Take care of the child called Ego in you.